Making informed
DECISIONS
inProduct Management

A book on Product Management, System Thinking and Human Behaviour.

NITIN MADESHIA

BLUEROSE PUBLISHERS
India | U.K.

Copyright © Nitin Madeshia 2025

All rights reserved by author. No part of this publication may be reproduced, stored in a retrieval system or transmitted in any form or by any means, electronic, mechanical, photocopying, recording or otherwise, without the prior permission of the author. Although every precaution has been taken to verify the accuracy of the information contained herein, the publisher assumes no responsibility for any errors or omissions. No liability is assumed for damages that may result from the use of information contained within.

BlueRose Publishers takes no responsibility for any damages, losses, or liabilities that may arise from the use or misuse of the information, products, or services provided in this publication.

For permissions requests or inquiries regarding this publication, please contact:

BLUEROSE PUBLISHERS
www.BlueRoseONE.com
info@bluerosepublishers.com
+91 8882 898 898
+4407342408967

ISBN: 978-93-6783-086-4

Cover Design: Aman Sharma
Typesetting: Pooja Sharma

First Edition: March 2025

Preface

Product managers make decisions that are pivotal to the organization. A decision made in silos can derail the organization and lose months of progress whereas a good decision can leap the team forward by years of success. In many terms, I feel this is one of the most important jobs of a product manager - to make good decisions. Hence, broader themes of the book are about making effective decisions. The decisions that you make as a product manager. It does not cover the basics of product management but is mainly targeted to help you evolve your thinking to make better decisions. I have tried to keep the book practical and relevant to product management by tying every concept with examples and resources. There are three parts to product management - what to build, how to build, and post release. You will find enough examples for each product role.

Major themes covered in the book are - system thinking, psychology, and finding the right solution through product experimentation. System thinking and psychology are lesser covered topics when we discuss product management but those topics have a massive impact on the overall product outcome. As one grows into a leadership role in product and business, these have a wider impact on the overall outcome of the organization.

The book starts with the customer because any business exists to serve a customer. It gives you a brief about customers, product metric, and overall prioritization to help you understand the basics of decision making. For an experienced professional or product manager, this is a refresher rather than a mandatory read. For a product manager who is just starting out or 2-3 years in the career, it would add enough value to bring up to speed to decision making. My assumption is most readers are already aware about these topics in some shape and form; hence I have tried to keep the discussion to a minimum.

Second part is where we discuss various system archetypes and their relevance in product management. Product managers would find this section insightful and thought provoking - how various systems are at play go unnoticed and have profound impact on the overall outcome. It covers topics from limits to growth, eroding goals, and fixes that fail among many others. I have tried to keep the essence of product management intact while dealing with system thinking. Examples mentioned provide a hands-on approach to thinking about various features and system design.

Part three of the book is how your customers think, and the psychology of product management. It has many concepts borrowed from the *Thinking Fast and Slow* by Daniel Kahnman and other psychology theories. My attempt is to help readers understand the impact from the point of view of product managers and business leaders. It helps readers understand how their user/customers perceive, interpret, and take decisions based on the information presented to them.

The final part of the book covers how you can design product experiments and validate product ideas. It follows a basic approach from finding the right problem to discovering the right solution and finally validating the solution.

Overall, the book helps you make better decisions in product and business.

Contents

Part I Introduction 1

    Chapter 1: Customers 2

    Chapter 2. Product Metrics and Data 7

    Chapter 3. Power of Data 17

    Chapter 4. Feature Prioritization 21

    Chapter 5. Product Manager Skills 30

Part II. System Thinking 35

    Chapter 6. Eroding Goals 36

    Chapter 7. Escalation 42

    Chapter 8. Fixes that Fail 47

    Chapter 9. Limits to Growth 52

    Chapter 10. Growth and Underinvestment 56

    Chapter 11. Shifting the Burden 58

    Chapter 12. Tragedy of the Commons 61

    Chapter 13. Success to the Successful 66

    Chapter 14. Law of Inversion 71

    Chapter 15. Network Effect 79

Part III. Psychology of Product Management 84

    Chapter 16. Biases in Product Management 85

    Chapter 17. Instantaneous Thinking vs Conscious Thinking 88

    Chapter 18. Law of Small Numbers 91

    Chapter 19. Representativeness and Plausibility 94

Chapter 20. Anchors and Science of Availability 100

Chapter 21. Regression to the Mean 104

Chapter 22. Cognitive Load 108

Chapter 23. Causes Triumphs Statistics 115

Chapter 24. Endowment Effect 119

Chapter 25. Prospects Theory: Decision Under Risk 125

Part IV. Experimentation 129

Chapter 26. Customer Support Tickets 130

Chapter 27. Launch a Training Programme 133

Chapter 28. Surveys 137

Chapter 29. Real-Time Interactions 141

Chapter 30. Customer Interviews 145

Chapter 31. Product Experimentations 154

Chapter 32. A/B Testing 158

Chapter 33. MinimumViable Product (MVP) 162

Chapter 34. Design Prototypes 165

Chapter 35. Beta Invitation 166

Resources 169

References 179

Part I
Introduction

Chapter 1: Customers

Start with the customer

Place the customer at the heart of every decision. Even if data trends and your customer support feedback seem to point in one direction, nothing replaces the raw insights gained from direct conversations with your customers. There is a lot you can learn from the customer - the obvious problems and the ones which are not so obvious. Even if you feel that your customer does not know what they want; you'll only get the idea of what they don't know after talking to the customer.

When I was in college, we had six subjects every year, each covering chapters from different books. Students often went to photocopy shops to get 5 or 10 pages printed for class. This problem became worse during exams when even the least attentive students needed notes. After the first year, we decided to solve this problem for ourselves.

At the start of our second year, we spent weeks in the library collecting books and marking chapters from our syllabus. We made the first complete course material for ourselves. We were our own first customers. During a conversation with my friend Nishant, we had an idea: why not sell these notes to our classmates?

Nishant talked to a shopkeeper who agreed to do bulk photocopying at 10 paise per page, while the market rate was 50 paise. We made the bundles and sold them at the market rate, making a good profit on our first few sales. However, we soon noticed other students using our notes without buying directly from us—they were getting copies made from the sets we sold.

To solve this, we started delivering the notes directly to our classmates. They didn't have to go to the shop and wait for an hour to get the photocopy done. They just needed to tell us, and we delivered. This worked, and soon every student in our class was using our notes. The convenience and simplicity of our solution made it successful, even if we didn't fully understand why at the time.

Around the same time, I was working at RCorp, building tech products for customers we never met. We assumed we knew what to build based on market trends. Projects with paying clients got completed, but our internal products were often stalled because we rarely sought feedback from potential users. This taught me an important lesson: when building a product, finding a customer is crucial. A customer helps you build the right product, brings energy, demands enhancements, and brings focus and accountability.

In 2017, I decided to start ArcMath (Math Edtech company I co-founded helping students become better at Problem Solving). I wanted to work in education but didn't have a clear idea of what to do. I had a lot of energy but no direction, so I pursued a course in mathematics education. Six months into the course, I knew what needed to be done. I formed a team and we started ArcMath on April 1, 2017.

At ArcMath, everyone had first-hand experience teaching students and dealing with parents. Initially, everyone became teachers with engaging presentations. We attracted customers by setting up one-day workshops to showcase effective teaching methods. Looking back, we were inexperienced, but our constant interaction with students and parents helped us learn and adapt, ultimately delivering what customers wanted and making a lasting impact.

In 2021, I joined TravClan, with ten years of experience in dealing with customers and building various products and services. Despite this experience, I struggled to understand the travel industry. I doubted my ability to grasp it, thinking maybe I only understood education. After six months, I realized I wasn't doing two crucial things: interacting directly with customers and engaging with the team that dealt with customers daily. Once I started doing these, I saw a significant improvement. Direct interaction with customers helped us address their issues more effectively and build the right products quickly. Understanding customer pain points and maintaining daily interactions with them clarifies what needs to be built.

Customers and product positioning

When you work with enough customers, you realize that no two people are the same. Hence, they will have different needs and aspirations in life. What is a problem for one person might be an easy task for another. This basic difference in human behavior, gives ample opportunities for a product to solve. Companies that succeed know that a single product cannot meet different needs for different kinds of customers. To do this, they adjust their products to fit the unique preferences, functions, and feelings of specific groups. By offering clear benefits to each type of customer, companies build loyalty and make it easy for people to see which product best fits their lifestyle.

Let's take an example of India's soap market of how similar products can still meet different needs and appeal to unique customer groups. All soaps aim to clean, but each brand highlights certain benefits that attract specific types of people. Dettol is well-known for protection and cleanliness. Its germ-killing qualities attract people who want strong protection, like families with children or healthcare workers. Lifebuoy also focuses on health but is aimed at a broader audience with its affordable price and strong family-health image. Medimix offers natural ingredients and Ayurvedic qualities, which attract people interested in traditional, plant-based solutions for wellness. This variety helps each soap brand stand out, making it easier for people to pick the one that best fits their needs.

Social media platforms offer another example of how products in one category can appeal to a range of users. Though all social media connects people, each platform draws users with unique interests. Facebook is popular for connecting with friends and family, sharing memories, and joining groups. It appeals to people who like staying in touch and being part of a larger community. Instagram focuses on visual storytelling, with photos and short videos that attract a younger crowd interested in sharing creative, eye-catching content. Snapchat is known for quick, disappearing messages and pictures, which appeals to people who want more privacy and spontaneity, especially younger users who enjoy sharing in-the-moment updates. Each platform attracts its audience by offering something unique that fits their online habits.

The car market also shows how brands can meet different needs, even while offering similar products. Tesla attracts tech lovers who are eco-friendly and interested in innovation. It's a luxury brand for people who care about sustainability and cutting-edge technology. Ferrari, on the other hand, is made for people looking for high performance and exclusivity. It's more than a car; it's a statement for those who want a luxury vehicle. Everyday cars meet the basic need for reliable transportation. These cars are affordable and convenient, aimed at people who care more about economy and dependability than luxury.

These examples show how the same products can be positioned to meet different customer needs. This approach helps companies make it easy for people to find products that feel like they're made just for them.

Understanding customer behavior

The success or failure of a company could easily be decided on their understanding of customer behavior. Suppose you have a food ordering application or a travel website for booking packages. You give users the option to search for food or find holiday packages. You suddenly realize that customers are actively searching for things you do not offer. This is a huge insight where customers behave differently than you expect. Rather than ignoring customer insight, it's time to act upon it to start reaping benefits and providing what the customers actually need. Such experiments lead to huge losses, but when customers deviate from expected usage patterns, their actions often highlight gaps in product functionality, reveal unmet needs, and even inspire innovative solutions. Twitter was initially created as a status-update platform, but users started using hashtags to categorize content. Twitter later embraced and optimized this behavior, turning hashtags into a core feature.

This is the power of understanding customer behavior. The path to building successful products always leads back to the customer. When we listen closely, their needs and behaviors reveal opportunities that data and assumptions alone can't provide. The customer should be at the center of product management.

Chapter 2.
Product Metrics and Data

Product metrics is the measure of how the user interacts with your product. But this is not the most important thing in product analytics. You need to know why your users come to your product. Most analytics is just a cranky set of data if the product manager does not know what value the product is giving to the customers. The answer to this is asking: what goals your users are hoping to achieve from your product?

1. Travel to another place
2. Entertain themselves for an hour
3. Split the bill between friends
4. Get fit
5. Feeling Relaxed and focused

Now each of these goals can be mapped to a product and ultimately a metric associated with them.

Goals	Product	Example Metric	Example Apps
Travel to another place	B2B Travel Platform	No. of flight bookings	TravClan
Entertain themselves for an hour	Video Streaming application	No. of shows watched or completed	Netflix

Split the bill between friends	Finance Planning App	The frequency of expense entries made by users	Splitwise
Get fit	Running App	No. of times a user runs in a week	RunKeeper
Feeling Relaxed and focused	Meditation App	Meditation session completion rate	Headspace

The metric that you use to measure the core value of your product is called the North Star Metric for your product. You review this metric every single day. This acts as your guiding principle for all the development efforts. You ask yourself, what will improve my North Star metric? Most of your initiatives start from here and trickle down to other projects to further improve the North Star. As the company or product grows, the need to track more and more metrics evolve. In order to cater to these evolving needs, Dave McClure presented a set of 5 core metrics to focus on product growth called Pirate metrics AARRR short form for Acquisition, Activation, Retention, Referral and Revenue.

In 2006, two Swedish entrepreneurs, Daniel Ek and Martin Lorentzon, founded Spotify with a mission to combat music piracy and make music more accessible. They had a bold vision: to create a platform where users could stream music legally and easily, without having to download or pirate it. However, turning this vision into a global phenomenon required a strategic approach that aligned closely with the pirate metrics.

User Acquisition was the first step. Spotify needed to get people interested in their product and attract users to the platform. They did this by offering a freemium model, where users could listen to music for free with ads, or pay for a premium subscription to get an ad-free experience with additional features. This model was appealing because it lowered the barrier to entry—people could try Spotify without paying anything. Spotify also focused on making the platform easy to access by launching in regions where music piracy was rampant, offering a legal and convenient alternative. Through these efforts, Spotify successfully acquired a large number of users in its early days.

Next came Activation. Spotify needed to ensure that users who signed up for the service had a great first experience that would make them want to come back. They achieved this by creating a user-friendly interface and offering personalized playlists like 'Discover Weekly,', which introduced users to new music based on their listening habits. When new users opened Spotify, they were greeted with an intuitive design and music recommendations tailored to their tastes. This personalization helped users feel an immediate connection to the platform, activating their engagement and encouraging them to explore more.

With users now engaged, the focus shifted to Retention—keeping those users coming back regularly. Spotify's success in retention was largely due to its commitment to continuously improving the user experience. They introduced features like curated playlists, daily mixes, and podcasts, ensuring there was always something new and interesting for users to discover. They also made it easy to create and share playlists, fostering a sense of community. Over time, Spotify's algorithms became better at understanding users' preferences, making the platform indispensable for music lovers. Users kept coming back because Spotify became their go-to source for discovering new music and enjoying their favorite tracks.

Referral was another critical component of Spotify's growth. Happy users naturally wanted to share their experiences with friends. Spotify made this easy by integrating with social media platforms, allowing users to share songs, playlists, and their listening habits directly to their social feeds. The viral nature of music sharing helped Spotify grow its user base rapidly. Additionally, they introduced family and student plans, encouraging existing users to bring others onto the platform. As more people started using Spotify, the platform became even more valuable, creating a network effect where users brought in more users, driving exponential growth.

Finally, Revenue was crucial for Spotify's sustainability. While the freemium model attracted many users, Spotify needed to convert these free users into paying subscribers. They did this by offering compelling reasons to upgrade, such as ad-free listening, offline downloads, and higher audio quality. Spotify also struck deals with record labels and artists to ensure a vast and diverse music library, making the premium experience even more attractive. Over time, as more users experienced the benefits of the premium service, Spotify saw a steady increase in paid subscriptions. This revenue not only allowed Spotify to pay artists fairly but also funded further innovation and expansion.

By 2023, Spotify had grown into one of the largest music streaming platforms in the world, with millions of active users and subscribers. The journey from a startup to a global leader in music streaming can be traced through the careful application of the pirate metrics framework. Spotify's ability to acquire users, activate their interest, retain them, encourage referrals, and generate revenue has made it a standout success story in the tech industry. Through this story, we see how strategic thinking, user-centric design, and continuous innovation can drive a product's growth and sustain its success over the long term.

Acquisition: New Users Over Time

The acquisition chart is a line graph that shows the number of new users acquired each day over a two-week period. Each point on the line represents the number of users who joined on that specific day. The upward trend in the line suggests that user acquisition is improving over time, possibly due to successful marketing campaigns, product launches, or promotional efforts. This chart helps product managers track the effectiveness of strategies aimed at attracting new users and provides insight into the best days or periods for user acquisition

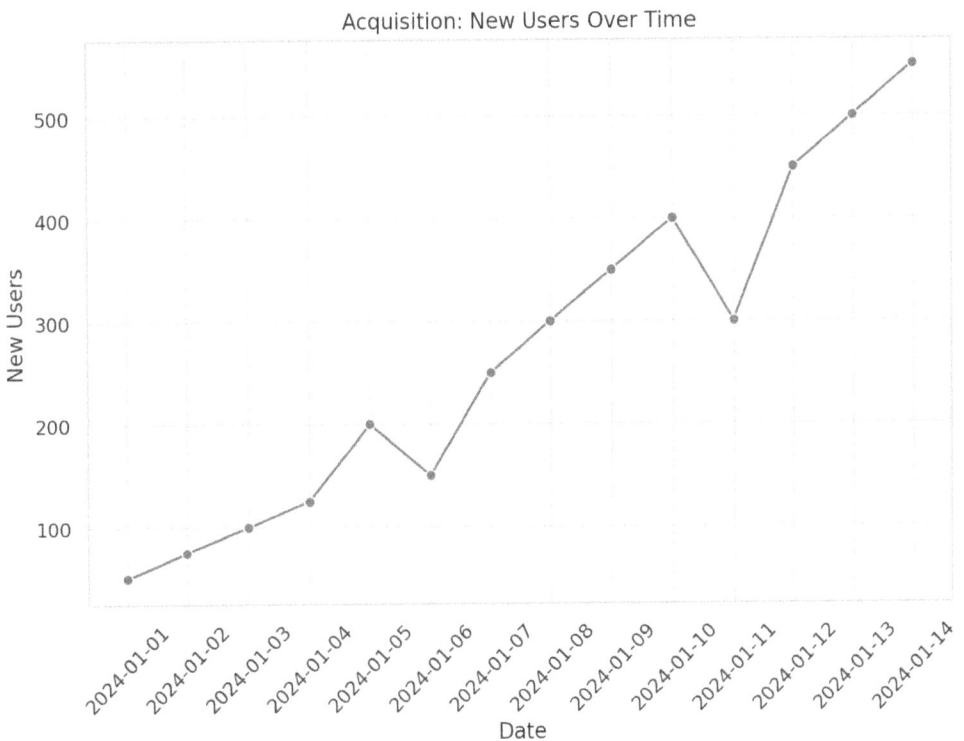

Examples

- E-commerce: Users visiting a website through targeted Facebook ads.
- SaaS: New users signing up for a free trial after a webinar.
- Mobile Gaming: Downloads from the App Store after a feature in 'New Games We Love.'
- Healthcare: Patients registering for a telemedicine service after a TV ad campaign.

Activation: Funnel Analysis

The activation chart is a bar graph that represents the user drop-off at different stages of the user journey — from sign-ups to the first purchase. The first bar shows the number of users who signed up, the second shows those who completed onboarding, and the third shows those who made their first purchase. The height of the bars decreases, indicating where users are dropping off. This type of analysis is crucial for identifying friction points in the user experience and helps in making informed decisions on where to improve the onboarding process to increase the number of users reaching the final stage.

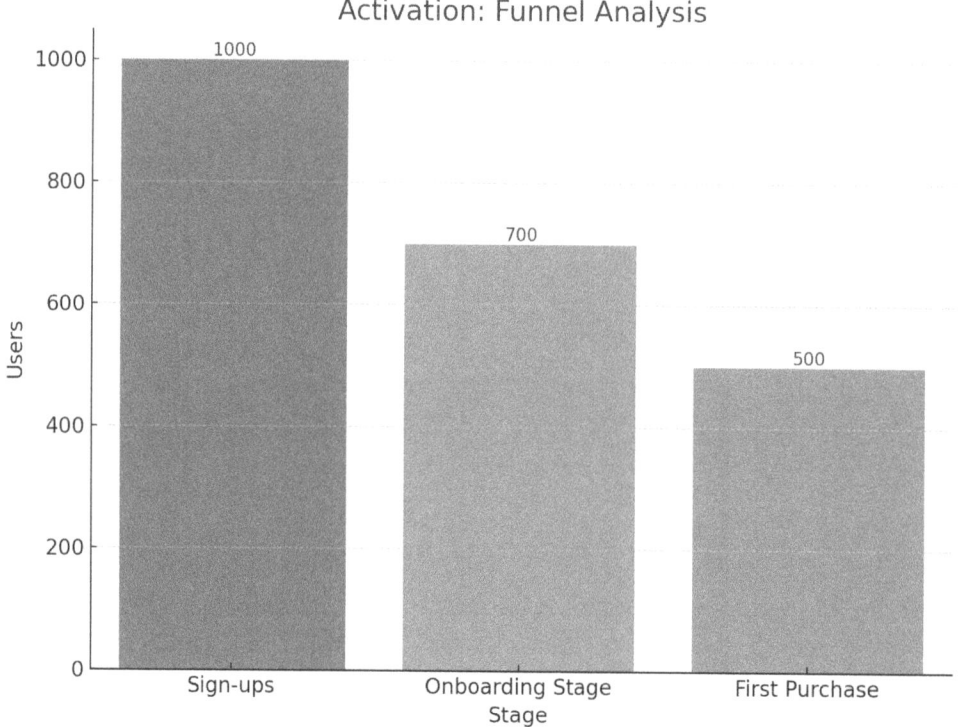

Examples

- E-commerce: Users making their first purchase.
- SaaS: Users completing the onboarding process by integrating the software with their existing tools.

- Mobile Gaming: New players finishing the first level of the game.
- Healthcare: Patients completing their first telemedicine consultation.

Retention: Cohort Analysis

The retention chart displays a line graph showing retention rates for three different cohorts of users over four weeks. Each line represents a cohort, with the y-axis indicating the percentage of users retained and the x-axis showing the week. A downward slope in the lines suggests that user retention decreases over time, which is common. However, comparing the slopes of different cohorts can provide insights into whether new strategies are improving retention or if there are persistent issues causing users to churn. This chart is vital for understanding long-term user engagement and loyalty.

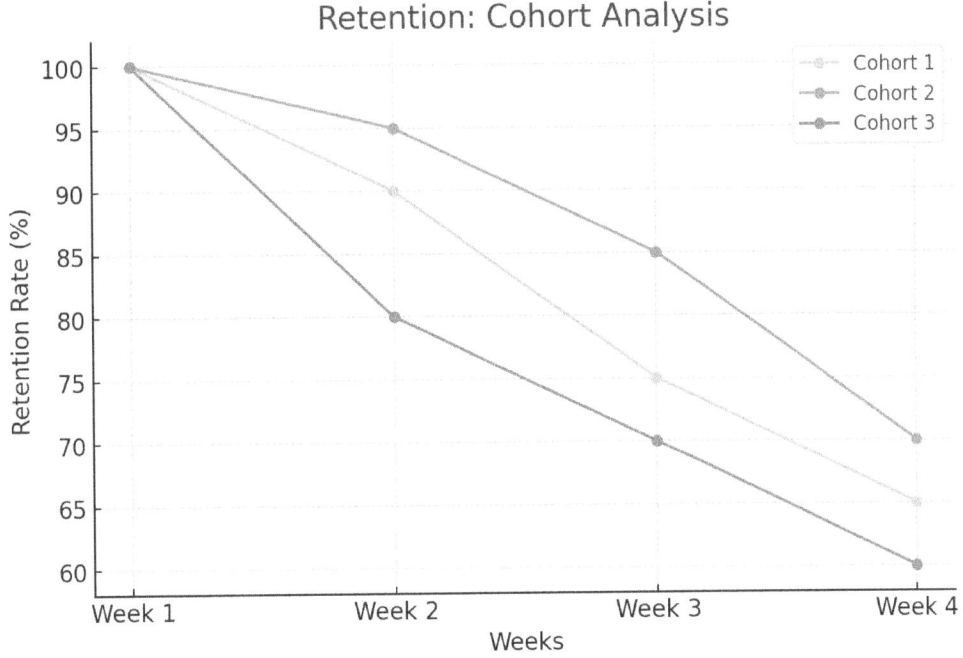

Examples

- E-commerce: Customers returning to make another purchase within a month.

- SaaS: Users logging in and using the service regularly after the first month.
- Mobile Gaming: Players returning to play the game daily over a week.
- Healthcare: Patients scheduling follow-up appointments using the app.

Referral: Referral Source Breakdown

The referral chart is a pie chart that breaks down the sources from which referrals were made, such as email, social media, word of mouth, and others. Each slice of the pie represents the percentage of referrals coming from a particular source. For example, if half of the pie is labeled "Email," this indicates that 50% of referrals come from email campaigns. This chart helps identify the most effective channels for referrals, enabling product managers to focus their efforts on the sources that generate the most user growth through referrals.

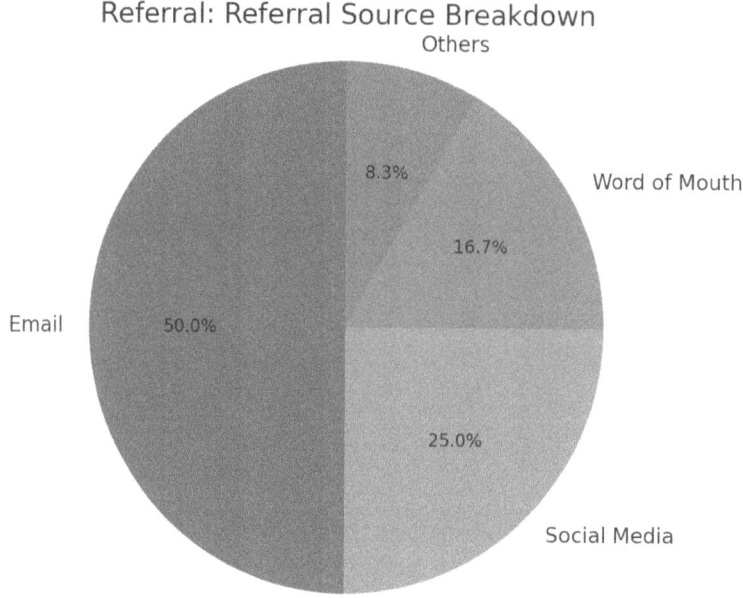

Examples

- E-commerce: Customers sharing a referral code with friends.

- SaaS: Users inviting colleagues to the platform via a referral program.
- Mobile Gaming: Players sharing the game link on social media for rewards.
- Healthcare: Patients referring others to the telemedicine service for a discount.

Revenue: Revenue by Source Over Time

The revenue chart is a stacked area chart that shows revenue over time, broken down by different sources, such as new customers, repeat customers, and in-app purchases. The y-axis represents the total revenue, while the x-axis shows the date. The different colors in the stack represent the contribution of each revenue source to the total. This chart allows product managers to see how revenue from different sources is trending over time, helping them identify which segments are the most profitable and where to focus future efforts.

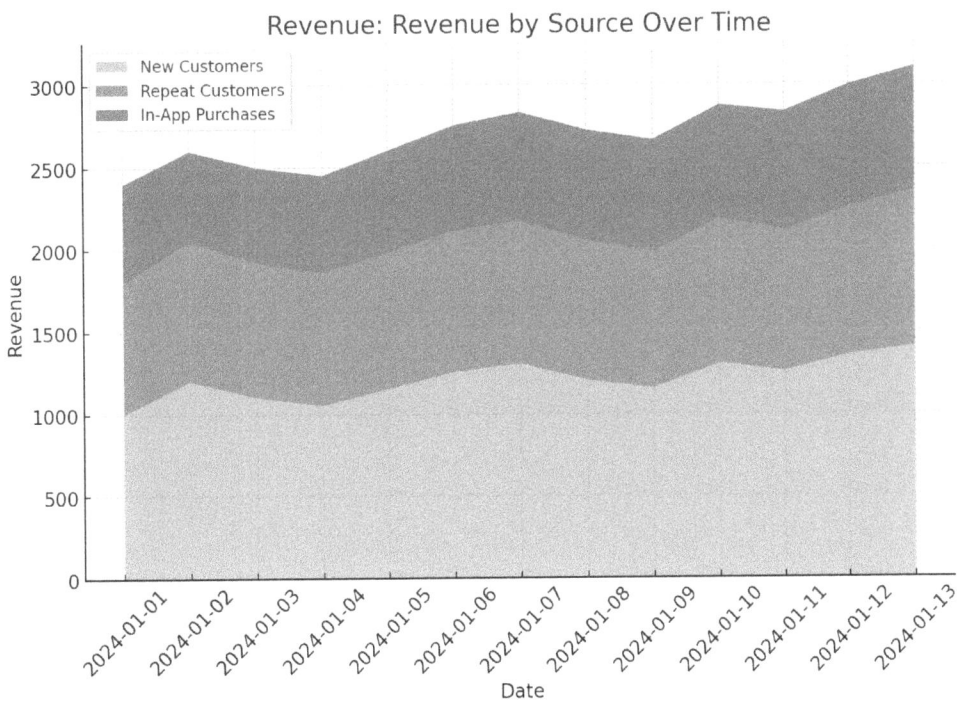

Examples

- E-commerce: Revenue from repeat purchases and upselling.
- SaaS: Revenue generated from converting free trial users to paid subscriptions.
- Mobile Gaming: In-app purchases of game upgrades or premium content.
- Healthcare: Revenue from consultations, subscription plans, and medication orders.

Now how do you track these major metrics for your product? Every product has some amount of user activities like sign up, add to cart, buy a book, search, etc. These user activities can be termed as Events. Tools like Mixpanel and Amplitude capture these events and offer you dashboards to create all sorts of advanced reports using these tools. How do these tools work? When you click, a button says 'Add to cart', your front-end system sends user id: 4353, time: 12:43:34, event = add_to_cart along with other device and demographics related attributes to these tools. Every time you click Add to cart, an event is counted and data is sent to these tools along with your information. These tools store this information in the database and present it to you in the report format when asked.

Chapter 3.
Power of Data

Data doesn't provide analysis; it simply answers the questions you ask. Just as project management tools like Asana or Trello are pointless without action, data is meaningless on its own. Success or failure hinges on how you use that data. The right way to move ahead is to create a hypothesis based on your learning. Then validate the hypothesis with running experiments. And then reiterate. It is only through running experiments and validating the hypothesis you make progress and bring innovation. We will cover more on experimentation in a separate section. What is more important is to understand data can be used not just for analysis but to drive user behavior.

One way to think about it is to move away from the conventional thought process of looking at data to find insights, and start looking at it as valuable information for your users – information they can use to complete a task. The rest of the chapter focuses on examples to help understand how data can be used to achieve user goals in different contexts.

Example 1: Health and Fitness

I have had many health goals over the years – trying swimming, going to the gym, practicing martial arts, and running. One problem that continues to haunt me to this day is staying consistent with my practice. I have never had enough motivation to keep going. I would start going to the gym and after a couple of weeks, begin questioning its value. Every day, I would wake up and question myself, "Why can't I do similar exercises at home?" Eventually, I would find it boring and stop altogether.

Over the years, I've been using an app called RunKeeper to track my runs. Spurts of motivation come and go, usually lasting only a day or two each week or month. Despite my inconsistency even with running, as time passed, more and more data got fed into the app. Slowly, I started feeling proud of my stats. I now proudly share my progress with my friends whenever we discuss exercise and health goals. I take pride in my first 5k run, my 100th run, my first 10k, and more. After using RunKeeper for many years, I upgraded to the paid version of the app and began training for various programs. My runs are all logged with different statistics: my personal best 5k, my personal best 10k, my longest run, and many other stats. This data has brought me back to running multiple times after months of gaps. It's like having a permanent resume that will stick with me forever. Data can create stickiness by generating emotional value over time.

Example 2: Food Ordering App

Another interesting example can be found in a food ordering app. Customers order from various places, and often forget the names of the outlets where they enjoyed a delicious meal. Features like 'recently ordered' and 'order again' are prime examples of using data to bring users back to the app. Imagine two friends chatting on a Friday evening. The user journey leading to a repeat order might look like this:

"That place had some great sandwiches."

"What was the name of the place?"

"Let me check the name on the app."

"Open the online store."

"End up browsing the whole menu."

"Craving for the sandwich increases."

"Let's order again."

The value of data and the convenience of repeat ordering result in another sale in this case.

Example 3: Flight Booking Portal

Booking a flight is not a simple task. Numerous considerations come to mind for a traveler:

- Are flight seats comfortable?
- Does the price fit my budget?
- Will I get preferred meal options?
- Do the flight timings suit my itinerary?
- What if I need to cancel or reschedule?
- Will the price increase if I don't book today?

Let's examine the user actions involved in booking a flight ticket:

1. Visit website 1
2. Log into the website
3. Search for flights with desired schedule (day and time)
4. Look for correct price point
5. Enter personal details
6. Check the cancellation policy
7. Review baggage information
8. See the final price with tax

This same process repeats for website 1, website 2, website 3, and so on. A close analysis of customer behavior reveals that they search for various flights and often abandon the process at the payment page once they know the final price. Users juggle through multiple websites and input travelers' information. To increase booking success, the product should streamline this process. Saving user information and preserving search history are examples that can help convert more customers. These features enable auto filling customer details or even resuming a booking, reducing customer cognitive load and drop-offs from the funnel.

Many human behaviors and decisions are spur-of-the-moment actions driven by the primal instinct to save energy, not necessarily money. Data can play a pivotal role in designing journeys that save user effort and cognitive load, leading to desired outcomes.

Example 4: Learning App

All learning applications face a common challenge – maintaining consistent learner engagement. Users often drop off after a few sessions or days. Numerous Edtech companies have attempted to solve this problem. I have been using Coursera for some time. Over the years, Coursera's interface has evolved to address issues related to learner motivation, consistency, and course completion rates. They have incorporated hyper-personalization into their product to enhance learner consistency and motivation. When you log into the platform, it prompts you to set your own goals. It then guides you in creating a personalized schedule, motivates you to complete courses, displays your course progress, and encourages you to stay on track.

If you closely observe, the common thread in all these examples is that all the data is generated by the user. It's something the user creates as part of their activities. It's information specific to that particular user. While many applications use this personalized information for marketing and business purposes, the true power for a product manager lies in becoming a data wizard – utilizing this information to fulfill users' goals, ultimately enhancing renewal and retention metrics. A skilled product person understands that this personalized information is a treasure trove on which adoption-focused features can be seamlessly built.

Chapter 4.
Feature Prioritization

A good product manager knows ruthless prioritization of product backlog. A product backlog is nothing but a simple list of all the features, issues, or ideas that you as product manager would want to implement at some point of time in the product life cycle. A product manager owns the product backlog and it is the responsibility of the product manager to pick the most relevant task.

Before thinking about different prioritization frameworks and techniques, it is important to understand why right prioritization is important. A company has fixed resources and if you are working in a startup, time is of great essence. A product manager cannot afford a sprint (15 days) on building something that does not get value or meet business objectives. Moreover, different stakeholders would want to prioritize different items as per their individual department goals. Hence delivering value is the most important work of a product manager and it cannot be achieved without right prioritization.

Let's understand what are some key business objectives. Most of your time will go in meeting certain key objectives and hence it is important that you have a clear understanding of these objectives. Ultimately everything in business boils down to earning more revenue. But more revenue does not start coming by just targeting sales in most cases. You acquire users, nurture them, get your first financial transaction, retain users and ultimately if your product is good, hope for the customers to refer more like them. This complete process is in more jargon terms a Pirate Metric - AARRR (created by Dave McClure, a Silicon Valley investor) - acquisition, activation, revenue, retention, and referral. These are five user behaviors that are strongly relevant to product growth. Now keeping in mind the business objectives, the product manager works on feature prioritization of the product backlog.

Usage to Effort or Value to Effort

Let us suppose the business problem that a product manager needs to solve is to retain customers by increasing user stickiness of existing features. It can be achieved by doing further enhancements in existing features. Simple answer would be to prioritize the feature with highest usage. But when we bring the dimension of time, the whole effort to reward dynamics changes. Below is the graph with Feature A, B, C, D, E and F in the product backlog.

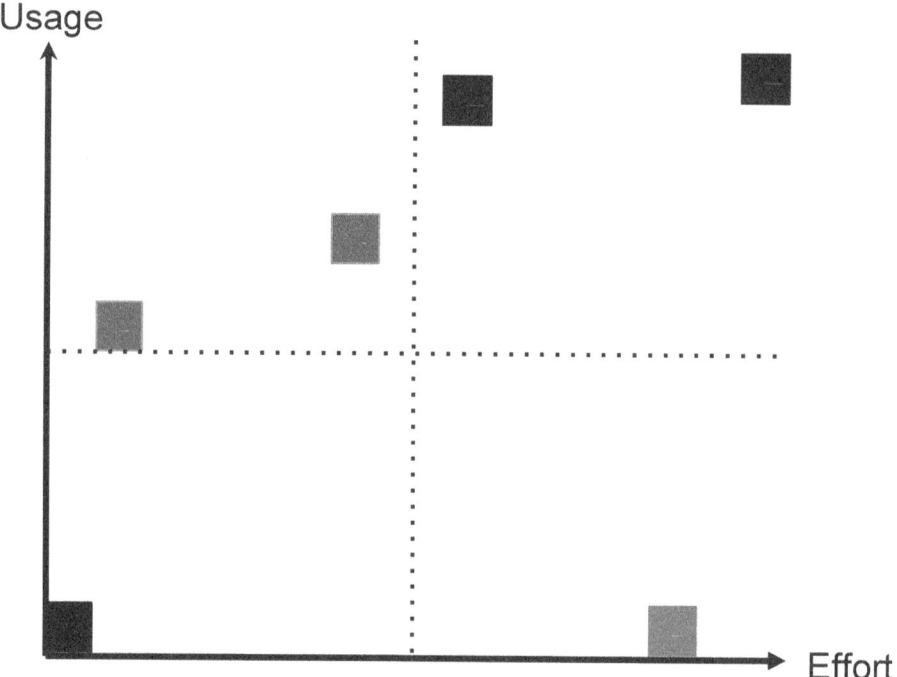

A, B, C, D, E, and F are features plotted on the graph with Development Time on the x-axis and Usage Frequency on the y-axis. Which feature should be prioritized for development? The assumption is that each of these features help in retention in some way or the other.

Feature A is a feature with least activity and least development time. Even though the development time is minimal this does not create any output as it being the least used feature.

Feature D is clearly out of race as it is least used with sufficiently high development time. This should not be prioritized.

Feature F This is the highest frequency feature but also needs a high amount of time. A product manager usually will go for this task when the value that can be derived is very high. It should lead to considerable business outcomes.

Between B and C, I would always go for B as the development time is marginally less and usage frequency is only relatively high for feature C. But in reality, we usually have the scope of accommodating more tasks in a sprint, hence it is easier to pick both B and C. Now finally deciding for Feature E is something that needs some weighing. In all such cases, we would go for features E only, if there is sufficient amount of confidence in the business output given the effort is high. Such features also get voted in case of a new business initiative or product strategies

Similar graphs can be plotted for **value to development time (effort)** and others. In case of plotting value, it is important to note that it will always be an approximate position on both the x and y axis. The idea is to structure your thought process and increase the confidence in the solution one is building.

Kano Model

The second framework focuses on enhancing customer satisfaction. Imagine building a business that customers dislike—such a business is unlikely to succeed. On the other hand, creating a product that addresses customer problems is essential, but simply meeting basic needs may not be enough to foster customer loyalty. This is where Dr. Noriaki Kano's insights become crucial.

As a product manager, your role extends beyond merely solving customer pain points; it's about creating experiences that delight customers. Dr. Kano identified that not all requirements contribute equally to customer satisfaction. His key insight was that customer needs can be categorized into five distinct types, each influencing satisfaction in different ways. Understanding these categories is vital for not just meeting customer expectations, but exceeding them and building lasting loyalty.

Dr. Kano realized that each customer need can be categorized into five different brackets:

1. Performance Requirements

These features are directly tied to customer satisfaction. Better performance leads to higher satisfaction. Worse performance leads to lower customer satisfaction.

1. **Internet Speed** (for an internet service provider): The faster the internet, the more satisfied the customer.
2. **Fuel Efficiency** (in cars): Higher fuel efficiency directly correlates with customer satisfaction.
3. **Delivery Time** (for online shopping): Faster delivery times increase customer satisfaction, while delays lead to dissatisfaction.
4. **Camera Quality** (in smartphones): Better camera performance increases satisfaction; poor camera quality causes dissatisfaction.
5. **Customer Support Responsiveness** (for software services): Quick and effective customer support enhances satisfaction.

2. Basic (Must-Be) Requirements

These are the minimum requirements that customers expect. Their absence leads to dissatisfaction, but their presence doesn't increase satisfaction.

1. **Cleanliness** (in hotels): A clean room is expected; dirty rooms lead to significant dissatisfaction.
2. **Security** (in online transactions): Secure payment methods are a must; any breach in security causes major dissatisfaction.
3. **Functionality** (in basic apps): The app should perform its basic function without errors; bugs cause dissatisfaction.
4. **Water Availability** (in homes or hotels): Running water is expected; lack of it leads to dissatisfaction.
5. **Basic Safety Features** (in vehicles): Seat belts and airbags are expected; their absence would lead to dissatisfaction.

3. Excitement (Delighter) Requirements

These features delight customers when present but don't cause dissatisfaction if absent. This is what they remember even after using the product or service.

1. **Complimentary Upgrades** (in hotels): Unexpected room upgrades create a memorable experience.
2. **Surprise Discounts** (in retail): Receiving an unexpected discount at checkout is a pleasant surprise.
3. **Personalized Welcome Messages** (in software or services): A personalized onboarding experience adds a delightful touch.
4. **Free Gift** (with purchase): A small, unexpected gift included with a purchase can delight customers.
5. **Exclusive Content** (for subscribers): Access to unique or exclusive content that wasn't expected can delight users.

4. Indifferent Requirements

These features do not significantly impact customer satisfaction or dissatisfaction. Customers don't really care about these features or services.

Their existence or non-existence does not affect the majority of your customers.

1. **Logo Color** (on a website): Most customers are indifferent to the specific color of a logo.

2. **Packaging Design** (for low-cost items): For everyday items, customers are often indifferent to packaging design.

3. **Extra Navigation Menus** (on websites): Additional, non-essential menus that don't add value.

4. **Social Media Integration** (in some apps): For certain user groups, integration with social media might not be important.

5. **Voice Assistant** (in basic mobile devices): Some users may not use or care about voice assistants.

5. Reverse Requirements

These features or services negatively impact the customer experience when present.

1. **Un-skippable Ads** (in apps or videos): Ads that cannot be skipped often frustrate users.

2. **Mandatory Surveys** (after every interaction): Forcing customers to complete a survey every time can lead to dissatisfaction.

3. **Overly Complex User Interface** (in apps): A complicated interface can annoy users and drive them away.

4. **Pushy Sales Tactics** (in retail or services): Aggressive upselling can drive customers away.

5. **Automatic Playing Videos** (on websites): Videos that play automatically when visiting a page often annoy users and can lead to dissatisfaction.

As a product manager focused on maximizing customer satisfaction, Kano's Model is an invaluable tool for categorizing requirements effectively. By using this model, you can prioritize features that fall into the Performance, Basic, and Excitement categories, ensuring they are included in your product roadmap. Conversely, you should consider removing features that are Indifferent or Reverse, as they do not add value or may even detract from the customer experience.

To accurately apply the Kano Model, it's essential to collect direct feedback from customers. Surveys designed to categorize features into these five categories—Performance, Basic, Excitement, Indifferent, and Reverse—allow you to understand what truly matters to your users. Engaging customers in this process is critical, as it ensures your roadmap is based on real user preferences rather than assumptions.

MOSCOW

MoSCoW is a prioritization technique for helping to understand and manage priorities. The full form for the same is **Must have, should have, could have, won't have**

Must Have: These are critical requirements that the project must deliver:

- The project fails or is canceled without them.
- They are essential for legal, safety, or usability reasons.

If there's no workaround, it's a Must Have.

Should Have: These are important but not essential:

- The project can proceed without them, though with some difficulty.
- Temporary workarounds may be needed.

Should Haves cause discomfort but don't stop the project.

Could Have: These are desirable but optional:

- Their absence has minimal impact.

- They are the first to be dropped if necessary.

Could Haves be included only if time allows.

Won't have: These are requirements which are not part of the project once identified.

MOSCOW is one of the simplest forms of prioritization. It often competes with other (simple) prioritization frameworks where Product Managers simply assign P1, P2, P3, or High, Medium, and Low. Moscow technique is successful in the sense that it gives meaning and definition to the prioritization exercise. Moreover, the relative priorities often create more confusion rather than quick solutions. Many product managers use the subset of framework when negotiating a particular requirement with the developers knowingly or unknowingly.

If you are working on a relatively bigger feature or project which has many user stories, the framework is particularly useful. The complete requirement should not have more than 60% of must haves else the risk of project failure highly increases. 60% ensures that there is enough breathing space in case of unknown surprises and the project keeps moving forward. I have personally found Moscow technique more useful during the sprint when a particular task is derailed. There is a new requirement that pop ups in the middle of the projects or some part of the task would take an additional day of effort and you would want to prioritize the scope. I would generally think from the user point of view whether this is a must have feature or could have. These are easy to know and help you make decisions faster.

Another place where the MOSCOW technique is useful is while validating your product ideas with the customers. You have tens of ideas for the problem you are working on. If you bracket the ideas in Must have, should have, could have, won't have, it becomes a lot easier to decide which solution you are going to test with your customers.

There are many other prioritization techniques readers are advised to read to further their understanding.

1. RICE
2. Story Mapping
3. Cost of Delay,
4. Feasibility, Desirability and Viability

While applying all these frameworks, it is important to keep the goal of prioritization which is focus on key objectives, time and resource optimization and delivering value to the organization.

Chapter 5.
Product Manager Skills

Solving information distribution

As a product manager, you are focused on gaining context within the company - of the customers, internal processes, decision making and much more. At the same time, you are required to solve for the flow of information, especially for your product growth. Information passing can be done by prioritizing it in the UI or through a marketing mailer. There are two ways you need to think about information communication. One is the basic communication with all stakeholders, be it marketing, business, sales, or the customer. Secondly, you need to think about how you design your product's features so that it itself becomes a medium for sharing information. Below, two examples from my own experience will help you to understand the importance of the flow of information more tangibly.

I was on a trip to Dehradun with my friends, excited and careless. After roaming through the city the whole day, we took an auto in the evening, put luggage on the back, and returned to the Forest Research Institute where our friends were studying. The auto dropped us off at our destination, and we got down and started talking about some random stuff. It was only half an hour after the auto left that we realized that we had not taken one of the bags out of the back. The whole atmosphere changed. From fun to sad to add to the problem, we did not let the security guards at the institution's gate note the auto details saying we were students from the university.

We tried looking through the city, but all in vain. We had a plan for the next day, and now, it wasn't going to happen. It was at this moment, late at night, we got an idea. We made around 50 slips on which we wrote about the incident and gave these to each auto driver we met for the next hour. We stopped the vehicle, explained the problem, gave them this slips, and asked them to give some extra slips to another vehicle they met on their way. We received a call from one of the auto drivers after about an hour saying that he had our bag. He returned to the college with our bag and one of the slips.

Another example was when one of the companies I was working with was part of a big industry fair, and we had several stalls in the hall. We wanted our customers to visit each stall. We created a small handbook called a "passport" and handed it to each of our customers. Customers had to get it stamped at all three of our stalls, and at the end of it, they would receive a gift voucher that they could use with our product. It was an instant hit, and we had customers swarming at all our stalls, and we would educate them about our services and offerings.

When I look at the two examples, a flow of information helped us solve those problems. What at one moment felt like a lost cause, suddenly had 100 auto drivers talking to each other about it. In the next instance, the customers had a goal, and we had a solution.

When I try to evaluate why it worked, I think of the following factors:

1. The paper slips and passport acted as a reminder. They were holding a tangible symbol in their hands and naturally had to act upon it.
2. The time we spent explaining the problem to each person conveyed the intensity of the issue at hand. We were able to create empathy in the driver's mind.
3. The small size of the city allowed information to spread quickly. If it were a big city, the problem would have died within 100 autos and never touched the source. There were fewer spots, or auto stands," where auto drivers met each other and talked about.
4. Gamification in the form of a passport, rather than asking customers to go to each stall, created an objective goal in their minds.

When launching a new feature, product, or service, if you can solve the flow of information, the chances of the product getting adopted increase exponentially. You must get it to sales, marketing, the on-the-ground team, the business team, and the end customers, all of whom are preoccupied with their problems and priorities. On the other hand, while designing the product, if you can identify points in the customer journey where there is an inherent need for communication, your product will grow. You only need to make the sharing of information easier for your customers. This is the reason why features like sharing on WhatsApp, sharing on Facebook, etc. work so efficiently. Sometimes, the new product does not get immediate adaptation. You need to solve for distribution. If you build a feature whose output has to be shared with anyone, it automatically has the property of distribution. When we solve the information distribution problem on a large scale, we need to reach a much bigger audience. That is why advertising, WhatsApp, or email marketing are such successful mediums for passing on information.

In fact, if you look at all human activities, we are just trying to communicate effectively and accurately. All software products are a means of getting or receiving authenticated information, be it for filing taxes or sharing a photo on Instagram. As a product designer, you need to focus on customer behavior that is repetitive and has a high frequency. The sharing of information qualifies both parameters.

Usefulness of useless information

A company has many moving parts that work together to achieve a common goal. You will know well about one function of the company, and the CEO will know about the many functions of the company. And that is where the difference is. A product manager should always be on the hunt for opportunities to contribute to organizational growth. Many of these opportunities often lie in plain sight, opaque to everyone. One sure-shot way of getting this knowledge is by being a lifelong learner and curious about every other function and job within the organization. Sure, it will take a long time, and you may question the utility of the information in the short term.

A product manager should build lots and lots of context, which over time accumulates to give deeper insight into the system. You'd know what most people miss, and what most people miss is a very fine web of knowledge that only those who care to see can see. The problem is never visible superficially, and the solution is usually simple. You need to be genuinely curious about everything that's happening all around you.

Let's take an example of the marketing function within the company. They are brainstorming on how to reach out to more customers. You, as a product manager, might find this conversation irrelevant to your job role as you are occupied with 100 other things in your backlog. By just being part of this seemingly useless information, you might gain some insight that affects your product market. One department will work to improve the customer experience; the other will work on acquisition; and the third will work to reduce churn and increase retention. All of these problems are interrelated. Moving one string has an impact on another.

This is not limited to other functions. You should know about other products in development within the organization. The consequences of these developments often have greater implications than are superficially visible. I made this mistake once. I created a feature flag that already existed for the finance workflow. The finance team never realized that a feature could be developed using the existing flag. They assumed that this was how it was supposed to work when I explained it. When it was finally given to the finance team, it added to their workload, thereby decreasing efficiency within the function. This problem went unnoticed until another feature needed that very same flag. They did not realize that they were doing the same work through two different workflows. I learned about it during a passing conversation. And I said you were using the wrong flag. One conversation led to another. It finally led to the root cause of the problem, and I realized the mistake I had made. I made two flags for the same process. This pointless conversation only resulted in significant improvements to a system that would otherwise have become cumbersome. Another time I got to know about the feature launch was in the sprint meeting. This feature affected another part of the product that was not in the impact areas. It stopped working. It is common for two features to share the same functionality, and any change in one can affect the other.

Apart from avoiding these errors, it is often useful to build a lot of contexts for the organization. It becomes easy for a product manager to drive results by having visibility into other functions, projects, and strategies. The more context you have, the more nuances you understand. And within these nuances, there are growth opportunities. For product managers who truly understand this, it is their superpower.

Part II.
System Thinking

System thinking is about seeing problems as part of a larger, interconnected system instead of looking at them in isolation. It focuses on understanding how different parts of the system affect each other and work together. By identifying patterns, relationships, and feedback loops, it helps uncover root causes and design better solutions. This approach is especially useful in dynamic situations where small changes can have a big impact over time. These patterns are commonly called archetypes in system thinking. We will discuss various patterns that are common and explore how these apply in product management.

Chapter 6.
Eroding Goals

The Challenger disaster on January 28, 1986, is one of NASA's most tragic and instructive events. Seventy-three seconds after its launch from Kennedy Space Center, the Space Shuttle Challenger disintegrated, killing all seven astronauts onboard. This tragedy was witnessed live by millions worldwide, making it a pivotal moment in space exploration history.

The primary technical cause of the disaster was the failure of an O-ring seal in the right Solid Rocket Booster. Investigations, including the Rogers Commission Report, found that management pressures, communication breakdowns, and an overriding desire to maintain an ambitious launch schedule contributed to the disaster among other factors.

Eroding goals archetype describes a situation when the initial goal that was set is lowered or compromised in favor of short-term pressures or goal leading to decline in performance over the time. This typically occurs when an organization or system, faced with difficulties in meeting its original high standards, lowers its goals to make them more attainable. While this may provide immediate relief or improvement, it ultimately results in a downward spiral as goals continue to be adjusted downward, undermining the system's overall integrity and success. The Challenger disaster is an extreme example of Eroding goals of safety measure but it sufficiently highlights its importance.

Let's take another example where a product manager is leading a team to create a new book reading app with a goal of providing a seamless reading experience. They have a tight deadline to launch it. The **Launch Date Goal** is ambitious, and as they get closer to the deadline, they notice a big

Deadline Gap — the difference between where they are and where they need to be.

The team feels the **Pressure to Increase Progress** and works harder to meet the launch date. They start making quick fixes and taking shortcuts to speed up. But these shortcuts lower the **Quality of Efforts**.

As quality drops, more problems come up, causing even more delays. **The Quality Gap** — the difference between the desired quality and the actual quality — gets bigger. The team then feels pressure to lower their quality standards to meet the deadline. This helps meet the deadline for now, but it harms their long-term goal of delivering a high-quality product.

Over time, the quality of the product gets worse, leading to unhappy customers and more work to fix issues after launch. The initial rush to meet the deadline ends up hurting the project's success. This situation is a typical example of the **eroding goals archetype**.

Let's see how different factors affect each other in this system. The idea is to only make the reader aware of factors or variables - launch date goal, deadline gap, progress, effort, time, and quality - at play in seemingly simple processes.

Interaction between Launch Date Goal and Deadline Gap

- Launch Date Goal sets a target for the project.
- The Deadline Gap represents the difference between the target and actual progress.
- A larger deadline gap increases the pressure to delay launch.
- Delaying the launch gives more time for progress on product, reducing the deadline gap.

Impact of pressure for Progress on deadline gap

- Pressure to increase progress arises from the deadline gap.
- This pressure boosts efforts devoted to launch.
- Increased efforts improve progress on product, reducing the deadline gap.

Impact of Efforts on Time & Progress

- More efforts devoted to launch can impact the quality of Efforts.
- The quality of efforts affects the time required to make progress.
- The required time influences the progress on the product.

Impact of pressure on Quality and Deadline

- The Quality Goal and Deadline Gap interact.
- Increased Pressure to Increase Progress affects the quality of efforts.
- Lower quality efforts can cause further delays.

These behaviors are easy to understand as isolated events but when all of the above factors play at the same time, it becomes complex to understand and leads to lower quality products. It often happens that it becomes the de facto behavior of the team under similar circumstances. Product managers should be aware of what is actually happening and take real-time decisions based on the current and long-term goal of the organization.

Let say the product manager achieved decent traction and engagement on the Reading App after the initial launch with some organic growth. Few months into the project, he faced another challenge when the pressure from the stakeholders to increase revenue surmounted. Due to pressure to boost revenue immediately, the app needs to find ways to generate more money in the short term. As a result, he, and other stakeholders resort to various changes in product flows and offering to meet business goals. It is important to note that unlike many other products where services are available offline, the reading application is itself the product that the customer is using. Any changes in product flow would not just impact the buying experience but the direct consumption of the product itself. When a product manager decides to double on the efforts to monetize the application, it might impact the long-term goal of providing a smooth reading experience. Below are some steps taken to meet the business objective.

Effort 1: Increased Ad Frequency:

The app starts showing more ads between chapters or pages. This results in immediate increase in ad revenue. But in the long run users find the reading experience disruptive and annoying, leading to frustration and decreased usage of the app.

Eroding Goals Archetype:

Show More Ads → Immediate Revenue Increase → User Frustration → Reduced App Usage → Long-Term Decline in User Base → Reduced Revenue over long term

Effort 2: Paywall for Popular Books:

Move a significant portion of popular books behind a paywall, requiring a premium subscription to access. This results in a short-term spike in subscription sign-ups. But in the long run free users feel alienated, and potential new users are deterred from downloading the app due to limited free content, leading to a decrease in overall user base.

Eroding Goals Archetype:

Move Popular Books Behind Paywall → Increase Subscription Sign-Ups → Free Users Alienated → Fewer New Users → Long-Term Decrease in Overall User Base

Effort3: Aggressive Push Notifications: Increase the frequency of push notifications promoting premium content, in-app purchases, and ads which in turn lead to immediate increase in in-app purchases and ad revenue. But in the longer run users become annoyed by the constant notifications, leading to app uninstalls and turning off notifications, reducing overall engagement.

Eroding Goals Archetype:

Increase Push Notifications → Immediate Increase in Purchases/Ad Revenue → User Annoyance → App Uninstalls/Turn Off Notifications → Long-Term Decrease in Engagement

Long-Term Consequences:

1. User Churn: Users abandon the app due to the intrusive ads, limited free content, and constant notifications.

2. Negative Reviews: The app's reputation suffers as users leave negative reviews about the intrusive and disruptive features.

3. Decreased Engagement: Overall user engagement decreases as the reading experience becomes less enjoyable, leading to fewer active users.

By focusing on these lessons, the reading app can avoid the pitfalls of the eroding goals archetype and build a product that remains valuable and enjoyable for users in the long term.

1. Ad Balance: Maintain a balance between ad revenue and user experience by ensuring ads are not overly intrusive.

2. Content Accessibility: Offer a mix of free and premium content to retain non-subscribers while encouraging subscriptions without alienating users.

3. Non-Intrusive Upselling: Use non-intrusive methods for upselling and promoting premium content to avoid annoying users.

Understanding the eroding goals archetype helps product managers avoid the long-term problems caused by short-term pressures. By knowing how the different parts of the project interact, teams can make better decisions that balance immediate needs with long-term success.

Chapter 7.
Escalation

"An eye for an eye makes the whole world blind." - Gandhi.

The Russia-Ukraine war can be analyzed through the lens of the escalation archetype in system thinking, where actions taken by one party lead to counter actions by another, resulting in an increasingly intense conflict. This escalation can be observed in the way the war has developed over time, with each side responding to the other's moves, leading to a cycle of increasing violence, international involvement, and global repercussions.

As the conflict escalated, the consequences became more severe:

- Human Suffering: Millions of people were forced to leave their homes, and many lost their lives because of the fighting.

- Economic Trouble: The war disrupted global trade, making things like food and fuel more expensive for everyone.

- A Stalemate: Despite all the fighting, neither side could win easily, leading to a long, drawn-out war that was hard to end.

The Russia-Ukraine war is a clear example of how escalation can make a conflict grow out of control, causing huge problems not just for the countries involved, but for the whole world. Understanding this helps us see why it's important to resolve conflicts early, before they escalate into something much bigger and harder to manage.

The **Escalation** System Archetype is a dynamic systems concept that describes how two or more parties or entities unintentionally escalate their actions against each other, often leading to self-reinforcing negative consequences.

In the early 2000s, personal computers were becoming commoditized, with Dell, HP, and Lenovo competing aggressively on price to gain market share. PC manufacturers continuously lowered prices, leading to thinner margins and cost-cutting on quality and innovation.

Instead of joining the price war, Apple took a different route:

- It focused on premium branding, sleek design, and superior user experience.
- Apple invested in ecosystem lock-in — integrating macOS, iOS, and iCloud seamlessly.
- The company built a reputation for security, exclusivity, and customer loyalty rather than affordability.

By avoiding price competition and emphasizing design, brand value, and seamless integration, Apple not only maintained high profit margins but also dominated the premium segment. Today, Apple is the most valuable tech company, while many PC manufacturers still struggle with low-margin businesses.

Similarly, in the cloud computing space, Amazon Web Services (AWS) initially dominated the market with affordable, scalable cloud infrastructure. As competitors like Google Cloud and Microsoft Azure entered the space, price wars became common.

Google Cloud tried to attract enterprise clients by lowering its prices. AWS also reduced prices selectively but avoided a continuous price war. Instead, it focused on expanding its services, adding features like AI, machine learning, and advanced computing. It also strengthened its offerings with enterprise-grade security, compliance, and exclusive partnerships.

By balancing competitive pricing with differentiated offerings, AWS maintained its position as a strong market leader without compromising profitability.

Let's take another example where a company uses a powerful Customer Relationship Management (CRM) tool to help manage interactions with their clients, track sales, and streamline operations. This CRM tool was designed to make it easier for the sales and operations teams to do their jobs and keep everything organized. Initially, the CRM tool was well-received. The product team, eager to improve the tool, relied heavily on feedback from the internal sales and operations teams. These teams had strong opinions about what features would make their work easier, and they were very vocal about their needs.

At first, the product team added some useful features based on this feedback. Encouraged by the success of this feature, the product team continued to add more customization options. The sales and operations teams kept suggesting new features they thought would make their jobs even better.

As time went on, the feedback kept coming, and so did the new features. While each new feature was intended to improve the CRM tool, the continuous influx of requests led to a problem. The tool started to become overloaded with features. Many features were rarely used, and some even caused confusion because they overlapped or conflicted with each other.

The Consequences

1. **Feature Overload**: With so many features, the CRM tool became cluttered. Users had trouble finding what they needed and spent more time figuring out how to use the tool than actually using it.

2. **Decreased Productivity**: The added complexity slowed down daily operations. Instead of streamlining processes, the CRM tool had become a source of frustration and inefficiency.

3. **Unused Features**: Many of the new features were not being used. They were added based on internal feedback but didn't actually address the

core needs of the users. This meant that the time and effort spent developing these features didn't translate into real value.

4. **Confusion and Training Issues**: The growing number of features required extensive training for users to keep up. This led to confusion and a steep learning curve, making it harder for employees to get the most out of the CRM tool.

What We Learned

- **Escalation in Features**: Internal escalation can occur when teams continually add features based on feedback without evaluating their true value. This can lead to a tool that is overloaded and less effective.

- **Balancing Customization and Usability**: While customization is important, it should not come at the expense of simplicity and usability. A well-designed tool should be easy to use and focused on the core needs of its users.

- **Evaluating Value**: Before adding new features, it's crucial to assess their actual value and relevance. This helps prevent unnecessary complexity and ensures that the tool remains useful and efficient.

The key takeaway is that more features do not always mean a better product. A balanced approach that focuses on essential features and user needs will lead to a more effective and user-friendly tool. Moreover, escalation strategies like price wars can offer short-term gains but often come at the cost of long-term profitability. If a company engages in an aggressive pricing battle, it may temporarily attract more customers but risks eroding its margins and financial stability over time. Apple avoided this trap in the PC market by focusing on design, branding, and user experience rather than lowering prices. Similarly, AWS strategically managed its pricing by offering selective discounts while differentiating itself through advanced cloud services and enterprise solutions. Companies that prioritize customer experience, product innovation, and ecosystem development can sustain profitability even in competitive markets. The key takeaway from Apple and AWS is that competing on price alone is rarely a winning strategy—businesses that emphasize differentiation and strategic pricing tend to achieve long-term success.

Chapter 8.
Fixes that Fail

Every winter, the capital city of India, Delhi struggles with the problem of air pollution. Multiple attempts have been made over the years to solve this, starting from the famous odd-even policy for vehicles and installing Smog tower at the center of the capital. The problem has persisted even today. The core problems are only in discussion but a handsome effort to resolve them haven't been taken up yet. Yes, there are problems in execution but more importantly have we resorted to fixing the root cause yet?

In product management, we often face urgent problems that need quick solutions. A customer complains about a bug, user engagement drops, or sales don't meet expectations. The natural reaction is to jump in and fix the problem immediately. While this can provide temporary relief, it might lead to even bigger problems in the future. This pattern is what systems thinkers call *Fixes That Fail*.

The *Fixes That Fail* archetype happens when a quick solution fixes a problem temporarily but creates unintended side effects. Over time, the original problem comes back, often worse than before. This could look like patching a bug in the app without addressing the root cause or launching a discount campaign to boost sales.

When we launched the OnTrip Application at TravClan initially, we focused on streamlining the communication with the travelers. All the trips were managed on WhatsApp where all communication with the drivers, support team and the guests happened. It was a brutally managed platform. As a result, the Ontrip App was launched but problems did not solve - drivers were still late for pickup, many tickets were not responded to on time. Now if we look in retrospect, the solution cries out on the face -

train support team for handling tickets and bringing discipline to drivers' pickup delays. Over time, we created a contract with Drivers on the delay policy and sharing the loss incurred due to bad experience. Similarly, more efforts were taken to identify what caused travelers to raise tickets and we started solving problems of safety, food options, providing support through local numbers, sim cards and many more. Ultimately support is only needed for a few concerns and if we keep solving the root cause, the overall Ontrip experience improves. Now, the team is shifting focus from solving issues to creating delight through Ontrip application.

In another example of fixes that fail - consider the problem of delayed refunds to the customers. The support recently reported the increase in queries and complaints regarding pending refunds. The same was reported to the team and the problem was diagnosed to be solved from the customer support team point of view. Since there were too many queries regarding refund, let's just create a dashboard for the users where they can see refunds status.

Users appreciated the new dashboard initially because it gives them visibility into the status of their transactions. They feel more informed about what's happening with their payments and why some might fail. Now this seemed like a good solution but if you look at the problem from the customer's point of view - they did not have the refund. Did the company solve the problem of refunds? No. The correct approach would be to find out the root cause of the problem.

1. Is there any operational efficiency?
2. Do teams slack over refunds?
3. Do we have proper tech in place to do faster refunds?
4. Are relevant teams empowered enough to make decisions?

At TravClan, when we faced a similar challenge, we created a simple button where the flight team could do the refund with a simple click of a button after verifying the case. It was both empowering the internal team as well as building products to improve customer experience.

Here are some examples of fixes that fail that are relevant for product managers:

User Engagement & Retention

1. **Boosting engagement with push notifications**: Sending daily push notifications to inactive users causes irritation and uninstalls, instead of addressing why users became inactive.

2. **Introducing gamification to fix churn**: Adding leaderboards and badges temporarily increases usage but doesn't address deeper usability issues in the product.

3. **Offering discounts to re-engage users**: A limited-time discount drives short-term user activity but trains users to wait for deals, lowering full-price purchases.

Product Features

4. **Adding a new feature for every complaint**: Adding features in response to every user request makes the product cluttered and confusing, leading to decreased usability.

5. **Launching a feature prematurely**: Shipping an unpolished feature under pressure results in bugs and bad reviews, undermining user trust.

6. **Copying competitors' features**: Implementing a feature from a competitor without understanding its fit creates confusion and doesn't solve core user problems.

Bug Fixing

7. **Fixing bugs with temporary patches**: Applying quick fixes to bugs without addressing the underlying technical debt results in more frequent failures over time.

8. **Increasing developer hours to reduce bugs**: Overworking developers causes burnout and lowers code quality, leading to even more bugs.

Marketing

9. **Overusing email campaigns to drive traffic**: Frequent emails temporarily boost traffic but lead to higher unsubscribe rates, reducing your long-term reach.

10. **Running aggressive paid ads to increase installs**: A surge in new users leads to high churn because the onboarding experience isn't optimized.

Revenue

11. **Introducing aggressive pricing cuts**: Dropping prices to compete with a rival boosts sale briefly but trains customers to expect discounts, eroding profit margins.

12. **Upselling without value**: Introducing upsell pop-ups annoys users when the promoted features don't address their needs, leading to churn.

Internal Processes

13. **Increasing meeting frequency to improve communication**: More meetings create short-term alignment but reduce productive working time, slowing progress.

14. **Switching project management tools**: Changing tools to fix workflow issues without addressing team habits leads to wasted time and frustration.

Customer Support

15. **Prioritizing ticket resolution speed**: Focusing solely on closing tickets quickly leads to poor-quality responses, which increases customer dissatisfaction.

16. **Offering refunds without investigating issues**: Refunds appease unhappy users temporarily but don't address the flaws causing dissatisfaction.

Team Morale

17. **Hiring more people to reduce workload**: Adding staff without fixing onboarding or training processes leads to inefficiencies and slows everyone down.

When you start focusing on the actual problems rather than symptoms you start getting more growth as a product manager. Always remember, the loudest cry does not always need to be the most important problem. As an exercise for yourself try to create a system diagram for the issues mentioned above similar to the one at the starting of the chapter.

Chapter 9.
Limits to Growth

One of the simpler ways to think about what to build next is not what (effort, activity, or feature) will get growth or improve the metric but rather think as to what is limiting the desired growth. This gives a very pragmatic lens as opposed to thinking about activities that will get growth.

The "Limits to Growth" archetype is a systems thinking model that describes a situation where exponential growth is limited by constraints or limits. It typically involves a reinforcing loop that drives growth and a balancing loop that limits growth when certain thresholds are reached.

Consider a fish population in a lake. The population of the fish cannot grow endlessly and due to constraints of space and food. Initially the fish population will start growing and more fish will reproduce. Over a period of time the amount of food available in the lake and the space available for the healthy survival of the fishes will become a limiting factor which will reinforce again and again. Let us visualize the example in terms of limit to growth archetype:

- Growth Driver: Fish reproduction.
- Reinforcing Loop: More fish reproduce, leading to more fish.
- Growth State: Population of fish in the lake.
- Limiting Factor: Availability of food and space.
- Balancing Loop: As the fish population grows, food and space become limited, which slows down the growth rate.

Every limit to growth situation can be defined in a similar manner in which a factor continuously acting leads to growth and another factor continuously acting as a balancing loop limiting growth. This archetype is common in many natural, economic, and social systems.

Key Elements of Limit to growth archetype

1. **Reinforcing Loop (R):** This loop represents the initial phase of growth where the system grows exponentially. The more it grows, the faster it grows, which can be due to factors like positive feedback, investment, or reproduction.

2. **Balancing Loop (B):** This loop represents the constraints or limits that slow down growth as the system reaches its capacity. These constraints can be resource depletion, market saturation, environmental limits, etc.

3. **Growth Driver:** The factor or factors that promote growth in the system.

4. **Limiting Factor:** The factor or factors that impose limits on growth when certain thresholds are reached.

Product or business managers will always find themselves in a situation where growth is plateaued. Understanding this archetype helps organizations anticipate and manage growth constraints effectively. For Netflix it is the increasing cost of creating and acquiring new content whereas for payment apps like Paytm, it is regulatory constraints that limit its growth. How organizations manage these constraints ultimately define their success.

In my first year at TravClan, I was involved in developing a B2B2C product aimed at travel agents. A key feature of this product was providing travel agents with a dedicated website integrated with a payment gateway. This feature allowed travelers to make payments directly on the agents' websites, fostering greater trust and reducing the hassle of money collection. The product, offered for free, perfectly matched the target market's wish list and quickly became a hit, with thousands of agents going live in a short span.

The product's initial success was driven by several factors:

1. Trust and Convenience: Direct payments on the agents' websites enhanced trust among travelers and streamlined the payment process.
2. Cost-Effectiveness: Offering the product for free made it highly attractive to travel agents.
3. Market Demand: The solution addressed a significant pain point in the travel industry, leading to rapid adoption.

We partnered with a Fintech company to provide the payment gateway services. Initially, the Fintech company had a turnaround time of about a week for completing the legal compliance and documentation required to activate the payment gateways. This timeline was manageable during the early stages of product adoption.

As the demand for our websites and integrated payment gateways surged, so did the compliance workload for the Fintech company. The volume of requests quickly exceeded their capacity, leading to significant delays. In some cases, the turnaround time extended to several months, becoming a limiting factor to our growth. This situation exemplifies the Limits to Growth archetype, where initial success creates conditions that eventually impede further progress.

System Analysis

1. **Balancing Loop (Growth):**
    - Action: Introduction of the travel agent website with an integrated payment gateway.
    - Result: Rapid adoption and increased demand for the product.
2. **Reinforcing Loop (Success):**
    - Action: More travel agents sign up, creating a positive feedback loop of success.

- Result: Enhanced trust and reduced payment hassle for travelers.
3. **Growth Driver:** Constant need to collect payments
4. **Balancing Loop (Limiting Factor):**
   - Action: Increased compliance workload for the fintech company.
   - Result: Delays in payment gateway activation, slowing down further growth.

To manage the Limits to Growth archetype effectively, it is crucial to identify and address the limiting factors early. Here are some strategies that could have been implemented:

1. **Capacity Planning:** Anticipating the demand surge and working with the fintech partner to increase their capacity for handling compliance and documentation.
2. **Alternative Solutions:** Exploring additional fintech partners to distribute the workload and reduce dependency on a single provider.
3. **Process Optimization:** Streamlining the compliance process to reduce turnaround time and improve efficiency.
4. **Communication:** Keeping travel agents informed about potential delays and setting realistic expectations regarding activation timelines.

This example shows how a well-functioning system can hit growth limits due to inherent constraints and how strategic improvements can help overcome these limits, leading to sustained growth and efficiency. Understanding and addressing limits to growth is crucial for the successful management and scaling of any system.

Chapter 10.
Growth and Underinvestment

In 1988, my father and grandfather started our family theater business. It took years of hard work and determination to set it up, especially in a remote town where navigating government approvals and legal hurdles was a challenge in itself. But once it opened, it quickly became one of the most popular places in town, shaping the culture of the time. For over ten years, people loved coming to watch movies, and the theater was a huge success. I remember some shows running full for more than a week, with excitement buzzing around town about the next movie. As children we always felt like an endless carnival was going on.

But as time went on, the world started to change. DVDs, VCRs, and eventually the internet made it easier for people to watch movies at home. We didn't invest in newer technology to make the theater experience special enough to compete with these options. We kept using the same old projectors and sound systems, and the gap started to show. Customer expectations increased but we did not invest enough to enhance the experience.

When we made some updates in the sound system, they were small and not enough to keep up with growing expectations. We improved a few things, but we didn't make the kind of changes that could bring people back to the theater. Fewer people came, and over time, the business started to slow down. Looking back, not investing into the business led to the closure after 32 years.

The **"Growth and Underinvestment" system archetype** describes a scenario where the growth of a system or organization is constrained because of underinvestment in critical resources or capabilities. This underinvestment creates a self-reinforcing cycle of decline or stagnation, even when growth potential exists.

Let's take another example at TravClan where we developed a website product for travel agents as mentioned in the previous chapter. We offered websites to travel agents at no cost, intending to use these websites as an acquisition channel rather than a direct revenue channel. It was a successful strategy to bring travel agents into travclan ecosystem. While many agents purchased these websites with enthusiasm, they often did not update them with necessary content such as packages, testimonials, or other relevant information. This often meant that the website was not relevant when the user visited. Also, from the travel agent's perspective, websites lacked features for SEO optimization and ads tracking. This lack of investment in maintaining and updating the websites led to lower renewal rates. In contrast, agents who continuously updated and invested in their websites saw higher lead generation. As TravClan shifted its focus towards revenue-generating products, the development and support for the B2B2C website products were eventually discontinued.

This can be analyzed using the "Growth and Underinvestment" archetype, which describes a situation where growth potential is limited due to insufficient investment in necessary resources.

TravClan provided websites for free, aiming to attract and acquire travel agents onto their platform. Despite initial enthusiasm, many agents did not invest time and effort into updating their websites. Now if we invested resources in the training of travel agents to update the website, as well as invested resources in further development of the website then it would have led to a more successful product. This is an ideal example of growth and underinvestment leading to a decline.

By recognizing and mitigating the factors leading to underinvestment, organizations can enhance the value of their offerings and foster a cycle of continuous growth and renewal.

Chapter 11.
Shifting the Burden

The **Shifting the Burden** archetype in product management occurs when a team consistently opts for short-term solutions to resolve problems instead of addressing their root causes. While these quick fixes may provide temporary relief, they often worsen the problem in the long run, making it harder to implement sustainable solutions.

In product management, one common mistake teams often make is relying on quick fixes to solve problems instead of addressing their root causes. The pattern synonymous to **Shifting the Burden** archetype. At first, it seems practical to patch up an issue quickly, especially when the pressure to deliver results is high. But over time, these temporary solutions can create bigger problems, making it harder to resolve the underlying issues. Understanding this archetype can help product managers and tech teams avoid falling into this trap and build sustainable solutions.

Let's consider a real-world example. Imagine a product team notices an increase in complaints about slow delivery times for their service. To fix this, they hire more customer support agents to handle the growing number of complaints. Initially, this works. The support team answers complaints faster, and customers seem happier. But the problem with delivery delays hasn't gone away—it's just hidden under the surface. The root cause, such as inefficient logistics or a poorly optimized supply chain, remains unsolved. Over time, the company spends more on support staff, yet complaints keep piling up. This is a classic case of shifting the burden.

The temptation to apply quick fixes is everywhere in product management. Another example might involve feature requests. Imagine users frequently ask for small changes to an outdated feature. To satisfy them, the product team constantly tweaks and adjusts the feature. These changes provide momentary relief, but they add complexity to the product. What the team should really do is redesign or replace the outdated feature with something modern and scalable. Yet, focusing on the root cause might seem daunting, especially when there's pressure to deliver visible results quickly.

Why do teams fall into this pattern? Often, the pressure to show immediate progress is a major factor. Stakeholders want quick wins, and teams feel they don't have the time or resources to dig deeper into systemic issues. There's also the fear of uncertainty — fixing a root cause might involve large changes that could disrupt the product roadmap or processes. Additionally, the focus on short-term goals, like meeting quarterly targets, can lead teams to prioritize immediate fixes over long term solutions.

However, relying on temporary fixes comes at a cost. It's like patching a leak in a pipe without replacing the worn-out section. Eventually, the pipe will burst, and the damage will be far worse. The same thing happens in products. Constantly addressing symptoms rather than causes can lead to increased technical debt, frustrated users, and even lost revenue.

So, how do product managers break this cycle? The first step is to identify the root cause of the problem. Tools like the **5 Whys** technique can help. For instance, if customers are canceling subscriptions, asking "why" five times might reveal that a confusing check out process is the real issue, not just a lack of features. Once the root cause is identified, teams can create a balanced plan. This might involve implementing a short-term fix to manage immediate needs while also allocating resources to solve the deeper issue.

Communication is also key. Product managers need to explain to stakeholders why addressing the root cause is essential for long-term success. For example, if increasing agent retention on a travel platform is a priority, the team might suggest improving the flow instead of just offering bigger discounts. A poorly designed flow can lead to lower retention even after spending thousands of dollars on marketing.

At TravClan, one of the reasons for lower retention in Holiday package products is the inaccurate itinerary. TravClan is at the forefront of innovation in the travel industry. While traditional DMCs operate within a single country, we've built a multi-country DMC at scale—a first in the industry. By integrating Agent Booking, Post-Booking Operations, and OnTrip, we've created a seamless system that enhances travelers and agent experience. Even though the flow is smooth, the inability to create and edit an accurate itinerary is one of the reasons that travel agents had low trust in the system and as a result don't come back. Another reason for the same is the product training which is required for each and every destination.

While discounts provide a quick boost, better onboarding ensures agents feel supported and are more likely to stay over time. Many a time product managers misjudge the core problems and decide to give discounts and cashback to achieve the desired result. The burden of completing the flow shifts from product to marketing and sales. This approach requires patience and clear communication, but the long-term benefits far outweigh the initial effort.

Avoiding the **Shifting the Burden** trap also means focusing on the right metrics. Instead of celebrating faster response times for customer complaints, a better goal might be to reduce the number of complaints altogether. By shifting attention to metrics that reflect the health of the system, teams can avoid wasting resources on intermediate measures.

In product management, it's easy to get caught up in short-term wins. But sustainable growth and user satisfaction come from solving problems at their source. By recognizing the dangers of the **Shifting the Burden** archetype and committing to long-term solutions, product managers can create products that don't just survive but thrive.

Chapter 12.
Tragedy of the Commons

India depends heavily on groundwater for farming, drinking, and industries, but unregulated use has caused a serious water shortage. Farmers often use groundwater to grow water-heavy crops like rice and sugarcane, supported by government subsidies that make pumping water cheaper, leading to overuse. Industries also rely on groundwater for their work, such as making products, bottling drinks, and cooling machines, often without proper limits. In cities, many households drill private borewells because municipal water isn't reliable, adding to the problem. Governments have focused more on quick development rather than creating strong rules to protect groundwater, which has made the situation worse. Together, these factors show how overuse of a shared resource can harm everyone and risk running out of groundwater for the future.

The **Tragedy of the Commons** is a systems thinking archetype that describes a situation where individuals, acting in their self-interest, deplete or degrade a shared resource, leading to long-term harm for the group and often for themselves. India's groundwater crisis is a classic example of the "Tragedy of the Commons," where various stakeholders—farmers, industries, urban households, and governments—have overexploited a shared resource.

In product management, the "Tragedy of the Commons" is a situation where shared resources are overused because multiple products or features rely on them. This leads to a decrease in the quality of the product or service, which can create a negative cycle. As these resources become stretched too thin, they begin to degrade, causing user dissatisfaction, and eventually, the system becomes unstable. This concept is not just limited to products, but also applies to many areas like businesses, social systems, and even the environment. In product management, it's essential to recognize when this archetype is taking place and find ways to manage it before it leads to bigger problems.

The "Tragedy of the Commons" starts when a company, or even a specific product, relies on shared resources, like a tech team, customer support, or a single data storage system. In the beginning, these resources are enough to meet the demands. But as the company grows and more features or products are developed, the need for those same resources also grows. For example, imagine a tech team that's working on multiple products at once. When each product starts demanding more attention, the tech team can easily become overwhelmed. As the workload increases, the quality of their work decreases because they are stretched too thin, which leads to bugs, slower development, and missed deadlines. This is where the "Tragedy of the Commons" begins. The shared resources—whether it's time, manpower, or technology—become overused and performance suffers.

Let's look at a feature at TravClan to understand this better. One of the features that the team has not been able to solve properly is the notification. At first it seems like an obvious feature with a lot of utility for the users. TravClan has multiple products on its platform with all different product managers. When the notification system was launched, the first product started showing notification which was very well received. Slowly more systems integrated and users were bombarded with notifications. The utility of notification for users decreased.

What we could do is create a unified strategy that organizes and schedules alerts to avoid overwhelming users. Ensuring that notifications are relevant and sent at the best times along with combining similar notifications into one. Finally, include feedback options so users can share their thoughts on the relevance and frequency of notifications. This input can help refine and improve the system over time.

Suppose a health app tracks basic health data, such as steps taken and calories burned, and provides personalized advice. Users are satisfied because the app is clear, easy to use, and gives them helpful health insights. However, as the app grows in popularity, more users sign up, and the demand for additional features increases. New features are added, such as tracking hydration levels, monitoring sleep, and logging dietary intake. At first, these new features seem like great additions, and they're well-received by users who want more detailed health data. But here's where the problem starts. These new features all require the same type of data: things like meal information, exercise logs, or hydration habits. Each feature asks users to input similar information, but without communicating with each other. Users end up entering the same data multiple times, leading to frustration. This redundancy creates a cycle of dissatisfaction as users feel overwhelmed by the constant need for data entry, and the effectiveness of the app's features begins to decline.

As user frustration grows, engagement with the app decreases. When users stop inputting data consistently or start ignoring the app's prompts, the app's ability to provide useful health advice weakens. Without reliable data, the features of the app, like personalized recommendations, also become less accurate. Users might start abandoning the app altogether because it no longer meets their expectations. This situation is a perfect example of the "Tragedy of the Commons." The shared resource here is the data, and because it is being used inefficiently by multiple features without proper coordination, the system as a whole begins to break down.

The lack of coordination among the features has led to user fatigue, inconsistent data entries, and a poor overall experience. The team needs to understand that if they don't act quickly to address the problem, they could lose their user base. They begin to implement solutions to streamline the data entry process, making sure that when a user logs a meal, that data can be used across all the relevant features. For example, when users enter their meals, the data is automatically shared with the dietary tracker and the health advice feature, saving them from entering the same information multiple times. They can also update the user interface to make data entry simpler and more intuitive, with autofill options and smart suggestions that make the process easier. These changes would help to reduce user frustration and improve the quality of the data being entered, which in turn enhances the effectiveness of the app's features.

With these improvements, the team can manage to fix the "Tragedy of the Commons" problem. By streamlining the process, they reduce redundancy, which restores the app's functionality and user engagement. This example shows that recognizing and addressing the "Tragedy of the Commons" in product management is key to maintaining product quality and user retention.

But how can a product manager prevent the "Tragedy of the Commons" from happening in the first place? The answer lies in strategic resource management. When different features or products start to depend on shared resources, it's essential to plan ahead and think about how these resources will be used over time. One way to manage this is by setting clear priorities. Instead of letting all products or features compete for the same resources, a product manager should assess which features provide the most value to users and focus resources on those. For example, if a feature isn't as critical or is underperforming, it might not make sense to continue investing heavily in it. Instead, focus on improving the most important features that drive user engagement and satisfaction.

Another important strategy is to continuously monitor resource usage. Product managers should be aware of how shared resources are being allocated and whether they are being overused. Regular evaluations can help identify potential problems early on, before they escalate. If a resource is becoming stretched too thin, a product manager can act quickly to redistribute resources, add more support, or prioritize different projects. This proactive approach can prevent the "Tragedy of the Commons" from undermining the product's success.

Finally, involving users in the process can help ensure that the product remains efficient and user-friendly. Feedback mechanisms are an important tool in product management. By regularly gathering input from users, product managers can identify pain points early on and adjust. For example, if users are complaining about the time-consuming data entry process, it's a sign that the system needs improvement. Collecting feedback helps keep the product aligned with user needs and expectations.

In conclusion, the "Tragedy of the Commons" in product management is a situation where shared resources are overused, leading to a decline in quality and user satisfaction. It's essential for product managers to recognize when this archetype is taking place and take action to prevent it from damaging the product's success. By prioritizing resources, monitoring usage, and involving users in the process, product managers can navigate the complexities of growth and ensure that the product continues to provide value to users. Understanding and managing the "Tragedy of the Commons" can help companies maintain high-quality products, keep users engaged, and sustain long-term growth.

Chapter 13.
Success to the Successful

The "Success to the Successful" archetype in systems thinking describes a scenario where resources or rewards are disproportionately allocated to already successful entities, often leading to a self-reinforcing loop that perpetuates success for some and failure for others. This archetype can be seen in various contexts, such as business, education, and social systems.

Let us see how this works in product and business

- **Two Entities Compete for Resources**: Two or more entities (people, teams, products, companies, etc.) compete for a limited set of resources (funding, attention, customers, etc.).

- **Success Breeds More Success**: The more successful entity receives a larger share of the resources, which in turn makes it even more successful. For example, a successful product might receive more marketing support, leading to increased sales and even more resources.

- **Failure Breeds More Failure**: Conversely, the less successful entity receives fewer resources, which can lead to a decline in performance, further reducing the resources it receives.

- **Reinforcing Loop**: This creates a reinforcing feedback loop where the successful entity continues to gain, and the unsuccessful entity continues to lose, potentially leading to a large gap between them.

Imagine a company with two product lines. One product is performing exceptionally well, while the other is struggling. Management decides to allocate more marketing and development resources to the successful product to maximize returns. As a result, the successful product continues to dominate the market, while the struggling product receives fewer resources, leading to further decline.

Sales teams across companies rely heavily on CRM to manage and optimize sales. During the product discovery process, the product manager finds out that the sales team needs to do more effective follow ups. As a result, they decide on two features:

1. **Email Automation** - Helps sales reps automate follow-up emails and campaigns.
2. **Lead Scoring** - Automatically scores lead based on their engagement and behavior, helping sales reps prioritize which leads to focus on.

Both features initially perform well, but the Email Automation feature gains more popularity among users because it directly saves time and has an immediate, visible impact on the sales process. As a result, the product team notices this trend and decides to allocate more development resources to improving and expanding the Email Automation feature. As a result, success to the successful archetype plays out:

1. **Increased Resources to Email Automation:** The product team invests more in enhancing the Email Automation feature, adding new functionalities like AI-driven content suggestions and deeper integrations with other tools.
2. **Decreased Focus on Lead Scoring:** Meanwhile, the Lead Scoring feature gets less attention. It doesn't receive the same level of updates or improvements, making it increasingly less competitive and less appealing to users compared to other CRMs that might have more advanced lead scoring capabilities.
3. **Feedback Loop:** Because Email Automation keeps getting better and more users rely on it, the user base grows more dependent on it. This success justifies further resource allocation to Email Automation, while Lead Scoring continues to stagnate, with users possibly even beginning to view it as outdated or less useful.

4. **Long-Term Consequences:** Over time, the gap between the two features widens. The CRM tool becomes known for its excellent Email Automation capabilities but is seen as lacking in Lead Scoring, which could be a key factor in lead conversion. This imbalance could lead to losing users who prioritize advanced lead scoring, or the tool could become overly reliant on a single feature, making it vulnerable if competitors launch superior email automation solutions.

Similar situations can be seen across products. Here are some examples across various products where the "Success to the Successful" archetype could apply:

1. E-commerce Website

- Successful Feature: Personalized Product Recommendations
- Neglected Feature: Search Functionality

2. Fitness App

- Successful Feature: Workout Plans
- Neglected Feature: Nutrition Tracking

3. Online Learning Platform

- Successful Feature: Video Lectures
- Neglected Feature: Discussion Forums

4. Ride-Sharing App

- Successful Feature: Driver Matching Algorithm
- Neglected Feature: Wait time optimisation

5. Email Client

- Successful Feature: Spam Filtering
- Neglected Feature: Inbox Management

6. Project Management Tool
   - Successful Feature: Task Management
   - Neglected Feature: Time Tracking

7. News Aggregator
   - Successful Feature: Trending News Highlights
   - Neglected Feature: User-Submitted Content

8. Customer Support Software
   - Successful Feature: Ticketing System
   - Neglected Feature: Knowledge Base Management

9. Online Booking Platform
   - Successful Feature: Last-Minute Deals
   - Neglected Feature: Loyalty Program Features

10. Productivity App
    - Successful Feature: Note-Taking Capabilities
    - Neglected Feature: Integration with Other Tools

These examples illustrate how a focus on the success of one feature can lead to the neglect of another, potentially causing an imbalance that could affect overall product performance and user satisfaction.

To prevent this kind of problem, the product team can take several steps. First, they should rebalance resource allocation, making sure that while popular features receive the attention they deserve, other features are not ignored. This can involve rotating focus between features to ensure balanced development. Second, they can develop a holistic roadmap by planning feature development with a long-term perspective. This approach ensures that even less popular features are updated and remain relevant, contributing to a well-rounded product. Finally, the team should establish user feedback loops to collect input from users across all features, not just the most used ones. Acting on this feedback will help the product better meet the needs of its diverse user base and maintain overall satisfaction.

Chapter 14.
Law of Inversion

While all the other mental and system thinking models help you identify the problems or understand the system better; law of inversion is where the innovation happens. Rather than thinking about what will get growth, it forces you to think about what needs to change or be avoided for the customers so that they buy more from us. This is different from Limits to growth. Limits to Growth explores the idea that exponential growth (in population, resource consumption, etc.) within a finite system (like Earth) is unsustainable. It emphasizes understanding and addressing the limits imposed by finite resources and the constraint of the variable within the system. The **Law of Inversion** is a problem-solving and strategic thinking approach where you consider what needs to change or be avoided to achieve a desired outcome. Instead of asking directly how to achieve a goal, you think about the obstacles and negative outcomes that must be avoided or reversed to ensure success. This method helps in identifying critical steps, mitigating risks, and fostering innovative solutions.

In the 1920s, the American Tobacco Company wanted to sell more Lucky Strike cigarettes to women, who weren't smoking much because it was seen as a man's activity. They hired Edward Bernays, who thought differently. Instead of just trying to sell cigarettes, he wondered what needed to change to make women want to smoke.

Bernays linked smoking to staying thin and promoted it as a healthy alternative to desserts. He got doctors to support this idea and worked with restaurants and magazines to make smoking a normal part of life. He also connected smoking to women's freedom, calling cigarettes "torches of freedom," and organized public events where women smoked openly.

Bernays's campaign didn't just sell cigarettes; it changed society so that smoking became a regular part of women's lives. His unique approach was about changing behaviors to make products more appealing, which greatly helped his clients.

Netflix is a great example of how using the Law of Inversion, can lead to huge success. When Netflix first started, their main goal was to become a big player in the home entertainment market. They initially focused on improving their DVD rental service by offering more DVDs, better prices, and customer service. However, this approach had limitations, such as waiting for DVDs to be delivered and needing physical storage.

Instead of sticking to this old method, Netflix decided to rethink the problem. Instead of asking, "How can we get more people to rent DVDs?" they asked, "What changes would make watching movies more convenient and enjoyable for customers?" This shift in thinking led to some major changes.

First, Netflix got rid of the hassle of physical DVDs. They began offering streaming services over the internet, so people could watch movies and TV shows instantly without waiting for DVDs to arrive. This made it much easier and faster for people to enjoy their favorite content.

Second, Netflix changed from charging for each DVD rental to a subscription model where customers paid a fixed monthly fee for unlimited access to all content. This made it simpler for customers and encouraged them to use the service more often.

Third, Netflix realized that people wanted a more personalized experience. They invested in technology to analyze what users liked and provided recommendations based on their viewing habits. This made it easier for users to find shows and movies they enjoyed.

Lastly, Netflix started creating its own original content. By producing exclusive shows and movies, they offered something unique that could only be watched on Netflix. This attracted new subscribers and kept existing ones happy.

As a result of these changes, Netflix transformed the home entertainment industry. The convenience of streaming, combined with a vast selection of content and personalized recommendations, helped Netflix become a leader in the market. Their subscriber base grew rapidly, and they became a major player in both entertainment and technology. Netflix used the Law of Inversion to rethink how people watch movies and made several innovative changes. By focusing on convenience, personalization, original content, and global reach, Netflix achieved great success and changed the way people enjoy entertainment.

Another great example is Paytm, the company who changed the way payment is made in India. Paytm launched its payment gateway service in 2012. This service enabled businesses to accept online payments through various methods, including credit/debit cards and net banking. The introduction of the payment gateway marked an important step in Paytm's evolution, helping it establish a foothold in the digital payments ecosystem and serving as a foundation for its later expansion into a broader range of financial services.

When Paytm first set out to dominate the digital payments market in India, they had a clear goal: make digital wallets and payment gateways the go-to alternatives to cash and card payments. Instead of adopting the traditional approach focused on promoting the convenience and benefits of digital payments, they realized they needed a different strategy to truly make an impact.

Instead of asking, "How do we get more people to use digital payments?" They flipped the question. They asked, "What would have to change in the customer's world to make digital payments ubiquitous and preferred?"

Solving Cash Dependency: One of the first things Paytm recognized was the heavy reliance on cash in the Indian economy. People were used to paying with cash for everything from small roadside snacks to large retail purchases. To address this, Paytm focused on creating solutions that could replace cash in everyday transactions. They worked hard to make digital payments a viable option for everyone, from small vendors to large merchants.

Wide Acceptance: Paytm knew that for digital payments to become practical and convenient, they needed to be widely accepted. So, they aggressively onboarded a vast network of merchants. They didn't just stop at big retail chains; they also brought small roadside vendors into their network. This wide acceptance meant that users could rely on Paytm for a wide range of transactions, making digital payments a more practical choice for everyday use.

User Incentives: To encourage people to switch from cash to digital payments, Paytm offered attractive incentives. Cashback, discounts, and rewards were all part of their strategy. These incentives made the switch more appealing and helped users see the benefits of using digital payments.

Ease of Use: Paytm also worked hard to make their platform user-friendly. They simplified the process of adding money to the wallet, making payments, and transferring funds. By making the user experience as smooth and easy as possible, they helped overcome the hesitation many people had about using digital platforms.

Trust and Security: Building trust was crucial. Paytm invested heavily in creating a secure and reliable platform. They implemented measures to protect user data and transactions, which was essential in convincing people to adopt digital payments.

Expanding Services: Paytm didn't stop at payments. They expanded their services to include bill payments, ticket bookings, financial services, and e-commerce. This made the app a one-stop solution for various needs, increasing its utility and user engagement.

Supporting Financial Inclusion: Paytm also focused on including underserved populations. They offered services in multiple languages and made the app accessible to people with basic mobile phones, not just smartphones. This widened their user base significantly.

Through these efforts, Paytm transformed the digital payments landscape in India. They became a leading player, significantly increasing the adoption of digital wallets and cashless transactions. Their user base and transaction volume grew exponentially, making Paytm a household name in India.

By using the Law of Inversion, Paytm identified the changes needed to make digital payments ubiquitous and preferred. Their focus on solving cash dependency, expanding merchant acceptance, providing user incentives, ensuring ease of use, building trust, and expanding services led to their success in transforming the digital payments landscape in India.

Here are some examples that would help you think through the lens of Law of inversion in varied context:

Scenario	Traditional Approach Question	Traditional Approach Answer	Inversion Approach Question	Inversion Approach Answer
Increasing Sales of Healthy Snack Bars	How would you increase the sales of a new type of healthy snack bar using conventiona	Increase advertising, offer promotions, highlight nutritional benefits.	Using the Law of Inversion, what obstacles or behaviors would need to change to make the healthy	Remove misconceptions about healthy snacks being tasteless, ensure availability in all stores, make them

	l marketing strategies?		snack bar the preferred choice for consumers?	competitively priced.
Improving Customer Service	How can a company improve its customer service to boost customer satisfaction?	Train staff, implement feedback systems, offer loyalty rewards.	Using the Law of Inversion, what customer service issues need to be resolved or avoided to ensure maximum customer satisfaction?	Identify and eliminate common customer complaints, ensure consistent service quality, avoid long wait times.
Promoting a New Mobile App	What steps would you take to promote a new mobile app to increase downloads?	Run digital ad campaigns, offer free trials, partner with influencers.	Using the Law of Inversion, what factors would need to change in users' daily routines to make downloading and using	Address barriers to app usage such as data privacy concerns, simplify the onboarding process, integrate the app into daily

			the new mobile app a natural and preferred action?	tasks seamlessly.
Advertising a New Electric Car Model	How would you advertise a new electric car model to attract more buyers?	Highlight features, offer test drives, provide financing options.	Using the Law of Inversion, what societal and lifestyle changes would need to occur to make electric cars the default choice for new car buyers?	Change perceptions about electric cars' performance and range, expand charging infrastructure, promote environmental benefits.
Increasing E-commerce Market Share	How can an e-commerce company increase its market share through competitive pricing?	Lower prices, offer free shipping, run promotions.	Using the Law of Inversion, what barriers to online shopping would need to be removed or	Ensure website security, simplify return processes, address trust issues with online payments.

			altered to make the e-commerce company the go-to choice for consumers?	

Chapter 15.
Network Effect

Network effect is simply defined as behavior of the system or the product whose value increases as more people start using it. There are two main types of network effects: Direct Network Effect occurs when the value of a product increases as more people use it directly. For example, a messaging app like WhatsApp becomes more valuable as more of your friends join it. Imagine if only two of your friends were on WhatsApp—it provides some value, but not much. When all your friends join, the value skyrockets because now you can communicate with everyone on the same platform. Indirect Network Effect happens when one group of users attracts another group, creating value for both. For instance, on Uber, more drivers mean shorter wait times for riders, which makes the platform more attractive to them. In turn, more riders make it worthwhile for drivers to stay on the platform.

Network effects aren't limited to digital products. One of the early examples of network effects can be seen in the railway system. In India, the railway network was so vast and essential that it used to have its own budget in the government until recently. If only a small number of people used the railway, it wouldn't be sustainable because of the high infrastructure costs. But because millions of people use the system, it holds immense value.

The railway system benefits from network effects because every additional station or route added to the network makes the entire system more valuable. For example, if a new railway line connects two previously unlinked cities, not only do those cities benefit, but the entire network becomes more interconnected, allowing for more efficient travel. Each station in a more general sense is a node which connects to another network. The more nodes a network has, the more successful it becomes. In products that depend on networks—like transportation or communication—the more connections you create, the more valuable the entire system becomes. Each network has a carrying capacity. Carrying capacity of the network limits the growth. As described in Limits to growth chapter, growth cannot be infinite; you will face limits to growth even in network effect. If more people join the network like the railways, it becomes a less popular choice of travel since it is overcrowded. Overtime people feel a sense of discomfort associated with their mind with respect to the network. Hence, the network cannot sustain infinitely.

The post office is still one of the most successful networks in the world. Much like a messaging app today, the value of the postal system grew as more people and businesses used it. In its early stages, a post office in a small village wouldn't have been very useful if there were no other post offices nearby to send mail to. However, as more post offices opened across the country, the network became incredibly valuable. You could send and receive mail from almost anywhere, making communication faster and more reliable than ever before.

The postal system was reliable and accessible, which made it a vital part of everyday life. However, much like the railway system, the post office faced a challenge: maintaining the infrastructure as the network grew. Larger networks come with higher operational costs, which is a key consideration for any product manager looking to scale. Even as new technologies like email and messaging apps have taken over, the post office still remains valuable, particularly for physical deliveries. Product managers must think about how their networks can adapt and evolve over time, just as the post office did when transitioning from letters to packages.

A network becomes indispensable when it hits a tipping point. Tipping point in a network is the point at which network effects kick in. Before reaching this tipping point, users may not find that much value in the product. This is one of the reasons why many products fail at an early stage even though they have enough network effect. WhatsApp is a prime example of how a product can scale through direct network effects. When WhatsApp first launched, its value was low because not many people were using it. A messaging app doesn't serve much purpose if none of your contacts are on it. But as more people adopted the platform, its value increased. You could now communicate with a larger number of people in your circle, and more importantly, you didn't have to rely on expensive SMS services. This is the power of direct network effects — every new user brings more value to the network, making it more useful for everyone.

WhatsApp hits the tipping point, the moment when enough friends of your group join WhatsApp. Before reaching this point, users may not find much value in the product. From the business perspective, WhatsApp required thousands of people to join the network. Once WhatsApp passed this tipping point, its growth exploded, with millions of users joining the platform to benefit from the collective value.

There is another example of a network which does not only depend on one type of user. As discussed earlier these are called indirect networks. Uber is an example of how network effects work in a multi-sided marketplace. Uber connects riders and drivers, creating value for both groups. The more drivers that join the platform, the faster and easier it is for riders to get a ride. This, in turn, attracts more riders to the platform, creating higher demand for drivers. Uber's product team works on balancing the supply of drivers with the demand from riders, a critical aspect of managing indirect network effects.

Uber's network effect is more complex than WhatsApp's because it involves two groups of users. If there are too many drivers and not enough riders, drivers won't get enough trips and may leave the platform. If there are too many riders and not enough drivers, wait times increase, frustrating users and driving them to other platforms. The key here is liquidity — ensuring there's enough activity on both sides of the network to keep everyone engaged.

Uber uses dynamic pricing (surge pricing) to balance supply and demand, keeping both drivers and riders happy. This is a valuable lesson for product managers working with multi-sided platforms: managing the balance between different user groups is critical for maintaining healthy network effects.

A very natural question, product managers would ask is how to build a product in the competing market where network effect has already taken over. How do you compete with established products like WhatsApp, Instagram? Each of these products mature and often lose the foresight that an overly crowded network will ultimately plateau. As companies build more and more features and move away from the simplicity of the product, it becomes annoying to some if not optimized over time. For example, Instagram feeds if not optimized will lead to irrelevant feeds often causing the users to leave the platform. You will always find the opportunity to tap into the underserved users with evolving behaviors. Overpopulation in digital products lead to decline in network effect. Too many feeds (irrelevant and not optimized) lead to users dropping. Too many notifications of friends' messages, etc. What is important is that the value or tipping for a new user should reach as soon as possible before the user leaves. If there is no initial adoption, it quickly starts to lose value.

Additionally, there are networks that need additional help from smaller networks. Delhi Metro needs a network of autos to help commuters reach the last mile. Look at the transportation system, you will always see an opportunity to create an additional network. You can still be a social media company and have clusters of brands pages on these platforms where your users come. Instagram cannot sustain on its own network rather depends on influencers to have an active following to bring their users. These examples of smaller networks within the network provide endless opportunities for businesses looking to explore network effects to grow their business.

Network effects can help your product grow rapidly, but they also come with challenges. Product managers must think about how to reach that tipping point where network effects kick in.

- Focus on Early Adoption: Like WhatsApp, you need enough users to find value in the product early on. Creating a seamless onboarding process and offering strong incentives for users to invite others can help you reach critical mass.

- Balance Supply and Demand: For two-sided platforms like Uber, balancing the needs of both user groups is essential to maintaining network effects. Product managers must use tools like dynamic pricing, incentives, and platform governance to keep both sides engaged.

- Expand Strategically: For physical networks like railways and post offices, expanding strategically is crucial. Each new addition must bring value to the entire system, whether by increasing connectivity or improving efficiency.

Network effects are a powerful tool in product management. From digital platforms like WhatsApp and Uber to physical systems like railways and post offices, understanding how to create, manage, and grow network effects is key to building successful products. Product managers must ensure their product is well-designed, easy to use, and capable of scaling efficiently to capitalize on these effects.

Part III.
Psychology of Product Management

As a product person, you need to understand why and how your user takes the action they take. You pass by a food joint and suddenly feel the urge to have food. Your friends tell you about their vacation and you too start having the thought of a trip. You see a discount on a particular product which even you don't need and have a sudden urge to buy. These thoughts are part of a person's desire, needs, and fear; all moderated through years of personal experience. The good part is you can learn to tap into these opportunities as a product manager to create products that are useful and successful. The hard part is it takes effort and needs a lot of iteration to reach an ideal solution. The next set of chapters deal with the psychology of product management.

Chapter 16.
Biases in Product Management

Product management is a field of decision making and product managers are prone to biases. It is almost impossible for a product manager to be unbiased working at the confluence of business, technology, and marketing. The chapter is chosen to be the first chapter in the psychology section so that product managers understand what is influencing their decision making before they understand what influences the user's decision. Biases in product management can lead to poor decisions and prevent teams from building successful products.

Confirmation bias happens when a product manager only looks for information that supports their beliefs while ignoring facts that don't. For example, they might focus on positive feedback about a feature but overlook data showing it didn't solve the problem. This prevents teams from seeing the full picture and learning what truly works.

Anchoring bias occurs when teams rely too heavily on the first idea or piece of information they hear. For instance, if someone suggests pricing a subscription at $100, the team might stick close to that number, even if research shows $70 would perform better. This can limit creative thinking and prevent teams from exploring better options.

Survivorship bias is when teams focus only on current users and ignore those who quit or failed to use the product. For example, designing features for loyal users while forgetting why others left can result in missed opportunities to improve. Understanding what didn't work is just as important as focusing on what did.

Recency bias happens when teams give too much importance to recent events. If a few users loudly complain about a bug, the team might drop everything to fix it, even though long-term priorities are more important. This can distract teams from bigger goals and lead to short-sighted decisions.

Availability bias occurs when decisions are made based on easily recalled information rather than accurate data. For example, a single loud customer complaint might take priority over a broader but quieter problem. This can lead to teams solving issues that seem urgent but don't affect most users.

The **endowment effect** happens when teams overvalue something they've already built just because they spent time or effort on it. For example, a feature that doesn't provide value might remain because no one wants to admit it was a wasted effort. This prevents teams from moving on and focusing on better solutions.

Groupthink occurs when teams agree with an idea to avoid conflict or stand out. For example, a team might push forward with a weak product idea simply because no one wants to challenge it. This stops teams from exploring different perspectives and making better decisions.

Feature bias is when teams think adding new features will solve all problems. Instead of fixing bugs or improving existing tools, they keep building more features. This often results in a cluttered, frustrating product that doesn't meet users' needs.

Overconfidence bias occurs when product managers assume they know what users want without doing proper research. This can lead to launching features no one actually needs. Overconfidence can be dangerous because it ignores real user feedback and data.

Status quo bias is the tendency to resist change and stick to what feels familiar. For example, a team may keep an outdated onboarding flow because "it has always been this way," even when data shows users drop off at critical steps. This can harm user experience and slow progress.

The **sunk cost fallacy** happens when teams continue working on a failing project just because they've already invested time, money, or effort into it.

For instance, spending more resources on a feature that clearly has no demand can waste time that could be spent on more valuable projects.

Negativity bias occurs when teams give more weight to negative feedback than positive. For example, if a few users dislike a new design, the team might scrap it even if most users liked the change. This can hold teams back from making improvements that benefit the majority of users.

Loss aversion is when teams focus more on avoiding losses than on achieving gains. For example, a product manager might refuse to remove an underused feature for fear of upsetting a small group of users, even though removing it would simplify the product and improve performance.

These biases can cause teams to waste time, make poor decisions, and miss opportunities to build a better product. To avoid these traps, product managers need to challenge their assumptions, rely on clear data, and test ideas before acting. By staying open to feedback and focusing on solving real user problems, teams can make better decisions and create products that truly add value.

Chapter 17.
Instantaneous Thinking vs Conscious Thinking

Instantaneous thinking is defined as the first response to an external stimulus. For example, when someone raises their hand in front of you, your automatic response is to step back a little. This is not a conscious thought. On the other hand, if you need to multiply two 2-digit numbers, it requires conscious thinking. Unless you have been trained to carry out multiplications quickly, the answer will not come *instantaneously* to your mind.

Example:

Below are the prices of various food items at a street food joint:

- Banana Shake: Rs. 50
- Almond Shake: Rs. 50
- Sandwiches: Rs. 57

Ravi went to a street food joint that is usually full of people. He ordered **2 sandwiches**. He went to the food counter to pay and asked the owner how much it cost. After about 4 seconds of delay, another customer, Jatin, walked in and asked how much he needed to pay for **2 shakes**. Surprisingly, the owner told Jatin the bill amount before responding to Ravi.

Can you guess why this happened?

You might quickly conclude that calculating the price of shakes is easier because the amount is familiar and stored in **reactive/instantaneous memory** through practice and experience. Another reason you reached this conclusion quickly is the current context of reading about instantaneous versus conscious thinking in this chapter. Our brains constantly look for tasks that require less effort and are easy to process. This is why the shopkeeper responded to Jatin before Ravi.

Another factor at play here is the **continuous flow of people** in the food joint, which allows very little time for each decision. The owner subconsciously prioritizes tasks that can clear the crowd faster, such as responding to easier calculations. But the experience of **Customer 1 (Ravi)** deteriorated because of the slight delay he faced and because he was given lower priority compared to another customer.

Based on this situation, what are two problems you can identify, and what are the solutions to those problems?

Problem 1: Delay in response time at the food counter due to a continuous flow of customers.

Solution 1: Implement a digital ordering system or hire additional staff to manage the crowds.

Problem 2: Inconsistent communication of billing information to customers.

Solution 2: Train staff to prioritize responding to customers in the order they approach the counter, and provide clear communication on billing information.

Let's Look at Another Example from a Digital Product. All products sold online include taxes. Consider the following customer journey:

1. User sees an ad on an advertisement platform.
2. User reaches the product detail page.
3. User makes payment on the payment page.

The question is: **Where should you show the tax information in this customer journey?**

We will evaluate the pros and cons based on the concept of instantaneous versus conscious thinking.

Step	User Mindset	Pros	Cons
Ad	Instantaneous thinking: Users act quickly without much thought.	Higher prices may signal better quality to customers with a bigger wallet size.	Higher prices may reduce clicks and result in losing potential leads.
Product Detail	Conscious thinking: Users evaluate price and other product attributes.	Users feel informed about taxes while considering the product. Phrases like "+ *taxes*" can be used.	Showing additional costs may lead to higher drop-off if users feel the price is too high.
Payment	Conscious thinking: Users fully focus on the total price.	Users may see the taxes as a standard charge and proceed with the purchase.	Users may feel deceived by hidden costs, leading to drop-offs if they are unfamiliar.

This exercise shows how understanding user thinking — whether instantaneous or conscious — can help product managers decide the right moment to share important information. By considering user behavior, businesses can improve their experience while reducing drop-offs.

Chapter 18.
Law of Small Numbers

EcoWorld produces eco-friendly cleaning products. During a strategic meeting with key stakeholders, the CEO, Jack, shares an idea for a new all-in-one cleaning solution. Jack had discussed this idea with a small group of customers at an industry conference, and they seemed enthusiastic, agreeing that it would be a great addition to the product line.

Jack presents the feedback in detail during the meeting, and based on the depth of this information, the team agrees to proceed with the new product. To ensure it's the right move, you as a product head run the idea by a group of sales and customer support team, who also feel confident it will succeed.

Convinced by this positive feedback, the company launches the new all-in-one cleaner. However, despite the initial enthusiasm, the product doesn't perform as expected in the broader market. The failure reveals that the initial feedback, drawn from a small, non-representative sample, didn't reflect the needs and preferences of the larger customer base. It was later discovered that customers have an unsaid choice for each cleaning product. They believed that bathroom cleaners have high toxic material whereas the kitchen cleaner used environment friendly chemicals. Customers in general have a mental model driving their preference for cleaners.

This outcome is a clear example of the Law of Small Numbers, - concept discussed by Daniel Kahneman in Thinking, Fast and Slow - where decisions based on limited feedback leads to an incorrect assumption about the product's success. The tendency of people to assume that small samples closely reflect the characteristics of the population from which they are drawn. This leads to the mistaken belief that small samples will have similar statistical properties to larger samples, which is often not the case.

For instance, if a few people in a small town win the lottery, people might wrongly assume that the odds of winning in that town are higher than the overall odds. People also tend to overgeneralize from a small sample. For example, if someone has a few bad experiences with a product, they might assume that the product is generally poor, despite it being successful overall.

Our group of friends used to visit a famous eatery in KalkaJi - a residential area in South Delhi. After covid ended, four out of seven of us visited the place. The other two went there on a separate occasion. Later when all of us met we somehow concluded that the eatery had lowered the quality of the food after Covid. Now this might be an over exaggeration of reality. None of us visited the place thereafter.

If you use a food delivery service and the order gets delayed a couple of times, you would readily generalize that orders are delayed when ordering through the particular platform. Few instances (sample) lead to generalization of the product and service. I have faced this overly in a product build for internal users. Whenever a small bug or interim server issue leads to software working slowly or some functionality not working properly, slack would be full of messages that the product does not work.

Another nature of small sample sizes is producing extreme results. Consider the below two statements:

1. Two friends at a party discussed the bad customer service by the cleaning company.

2. In a survey conducted with around 1000 people it was found that 37% of them are not satisfied with the customer service of the cleaning company.

In the above example, statement one is an example of extremity displayed by small samples whereas statement 2 normalizes the impact of statement 1 and presents a clearer picture of the company's customer service. The larger the sample size, the more reliable the data, as it better reflects the true characteristics of the population.

Product managers are highly prone to mistakes in decision making based on the opinion of few people in the organization. These people are highly vocal about their problem and will convey the same like it's the end of the world for them until an action is taken. Focusing too much on such issues leads to achieving local maxima or incorrect prioritization. Relying on small numbers can lead to flawed decisions and judgments. In order to capture the preference of customers accurately, larger sample sizes should be used.

Chapter 19.
Representativeness and Plausibility

Daniel Kahneman, in his book *Thinking, Fast and Slow*, explains how our minds use intuitive thinking to make quick judgments based on two key concepts: "representation" and "plausibility." Representation is about how information is presented to us, while plausibility is about how believable that information seems.

Imagine you're looking at two images of tea brands and are asked to choose the healthier option.

Image 1

Image 2

Both brands use a green leaf on their packaging to represent the tea's healthy nature. One might emphasize the word "antioxidant," while another might use "antioxidant" along with "health," a term many people associate with wellness. These visual cues and words tap into our minds' tendency to make snap judgments. Most people would likely choose the second option, as it uses representation more effectively to signal healthiness, even if both teas are similar in reality.

This idea of representation also appears in branding. A friend of mine started a snack brand called *HealthyFirst*, selling products like roasted almonds dipped in chocolate and sugar-coated cashews. The name *HealthyFirst* makes people think the snacks are good for them, even though the actual products might not be as healthy as they seem. This is a common strategy in the food industry, where brands use names and images that represent health to influence our choices, even if the products themselves aren't particularly healthy.

In the digital world, representation plays a big role in how we perceive product features. For example, when an app displays a verified icon or a lock symbol, it signals trust and security. If a payment service says it's "Brand X Verified," it might not mean much. But if it's "Paytm Verified" or "Apple Verified" with the familiar logos, it instantly creates a feeling of trust because these brands have built a strong reputation over time.

Google Maps offers another example. When you use it to check traffic, it shows green, yellow, or red lines to represent different traffic conditions. These colors are easy to understand because they align with the traffic lights, we see every day. This representation makes the information on Google Maps instantly clear and useful.

But it's not just about representation; plausibility also matters. When Google Maps shows the estimated time to reach a destination, most people believe it's accurate because it matches their real-world experience. Similarly, apps like Uber or Delhi Metro provide estimated arrival times. Even if a cab gets delayed or a train's arrival time changes, users still trust these estimates because they generally align with what they expect.

Plausibility is also crucial for security features, like WhatsApp's end-to-end encryption. This feature promises that only the sender and recipient can read messages, which aligns with users' expectations of privacy. WhatsApp reinforces this by displaying a message that confirms chats are encrypted, making the promise of privacy more believable and trustworthy.

Representation and plausibility are also powerful tools in advertising and on landing pages. Consider a travel package ad featuring a tropical beach, a plane ticket, and a bold "50% OFF" label. These visuals represent relaxation and a great deal, making the ad instantly relatable. When users click the ad and land on a page with more images of the destination, a countdown timer, and clear pricing, they are more likely to book because the page represents the vacation experience they desire.

Similarly, an ad for a discounted smartphone might include a testimonial from a happy customer to make the offer more plausible. When users click through to the product listing, they see detailed specifications, reviews, and a clear explanation of the discount, which builds trust. The combination of strong representation and plausibility encourages users to make a purchase.

In conclusion, by applying the concepts of representation and plausibility in marketing and product development, businesses can create more effective strategies. Representation ensures that visuals and layouts are intuitive and relatable, while plausibility makes the offers seem credible and trustworthy. This combination drives user engagement, leading to actions like clicking on ads, exploring landing pages, or making purchases.

Here are 10 exercises designed to help you understand and apply the concepts of representation and plausibility. These exercises encourage critical thinking and practical application of the concepts in real-world scenarios.

Exercise 1: Identifying Representation in Branding Objective: Identify how brands use visual representation to convey a message. **Task:** Look at five different food products in your kitchen. Analyze the packaging and identify the visual elements (like colors, symbols, or images) that the brand uses to represent healthiness, freshness, or quality. Write down what each element represents and how it influences your perception of the product.

Exercise 2: Plausibility in Product Descriptions

Objective: Assess the plausibility of product claims.
Task: Visit an e-commerce website and choose three different products with promotional descriptions (e.g., "Best-selling," "Limited Time Offer," "Scientifically Proven"). Evaluate each claim for plausibility. Consider what makes these claims believable or not, and write down your thoughts.

Exercise 3: Designing a Plausible Advertisement Objective:

Create an ad that uses plausibility to build trust.
Task: Imagine you are marketing a new fitness app. Design an advertisement that includes at least two elements to make the app's benefits seem plausible (e.g., testimonials, before-and-after photos, or scientific data). Explain why these elements make the ad more believable.

Exercise 4: Representation in User Interface (UI) Design Objective:

Analyze how representation is used in digital products.
Task: Choose a popular app (e.g., WhatsApp, Instagram, or Uber) and identify three UI elements that use representation to convey meaning (e.g., icons, colors, or layout). Describe what each element represents and how it contributes to the user experience.

Exercise 5: Plausibility and Pricing Strategies Objective:

Explore how pricing strategies use plausibility.
Task: Think of a recent purchase you made during a sale. Reflect on the pricing strategy used (e.g., "Buy One, Get One Free," "50% Off," "Limited Time Discount"). Analyze why you found the discount plausible. Write a brief explanation of what made the deal believable.

Exercise 6: Representation in social media Objective:

Understand how social media posts use representation.
Task: Scroll through your social media feed and select three posts that use

visuals to represent ideas (e.g., a charity using images of children to represent need, or a fitness influencer using workout videos to represent health). Describe how each post uses representation to convey its message and influence the viewer.

Exercise 7: Testing Plausibility with Counter-Examples

Objective: Challenge the plausibility of a claim by providing a counter-example.
Task: Find a product advertisement that makes a bold claim (e.g., "The Best Laptop in the World"). Create a counter-example or scenario that challenges the plausibility of this claim. Write down how this counter-example affects your trust in the original claim.

Exercise 8: Representation in Product Packaging

Objective: Redesign product packaging using representation.
Task: Take a common household product (e.g., toothpaste, cereal, or detergent) and redesign its packaging to represent a different attribute (e.g., eco-friendliness, luxury, or affordability). Draw or describe your new design and explain how the changes in representation could influence consumer perception.

Exercise 9: Plausibility in News Headlines

Objective: Evaluate the plausibility of news headlines.
Task: Find three news headlines from different sources. Analyze the plausibility of each headline by considering the source's credibility, the content of the headline, and your own knowledge of the topic. Rank the headlines from most to least plausible and explain your reasoning.

Exercise 10: Role-Playing Plausibility in Customer Service

Objective: Practice using plausibility in customer communication.
Task: Role-play a scenario where you are a customer service representative for a tech company. A customer doubts the security of your product. Create a dialogue where you use plausible arguments (e.g., mentioning

certifications, reviews, or security features) to reassure the customer. Write down the dialogue and reflect on how your arguments enhanced the product's credibility.

These exercises can be used individually or in group settings to deepen understanding of representation and plausibility. Each task encourages you to apply these concepts in various contexts, helping you develop skills that are directly relevant to product management and decision-making.

Chapter 20.
Anchors and Science of Availability

Anchoring is a cognitive bias where individuals rely heavily on the first piece of information they encounter (the "anchor") when making decisions. This initial reference point sets the tone for subsequent judgments and decisions, often leading to biased outcomes. For instance, imagine you're shopping for a car, and the first car you see is priced at $30,000. Even if the next cars you view are cheaper, you might still perceive them as better deals relative to the $30,000 anchor.

Anchors can take the form of numbers, values, or any initial piece of information presented at the start of a decision-making process. Interestingly, even arbitrary, or irrelevant anchors can significantly influence judgments. After exposure to an anchor, people tend to adjust their estimates or decisions away from it. However, these adjustments are usually insufficient, causing their final judgments to remain biased toward the anchor.

Anchoring influences various areas, including pricing, negotiations, probability estimates, and self-assessments. For example, during salary negotiations, the first number mentioned often sets the tone for the entire discussion, heavily influencing the final agreement.

Product managers can use the concept of anchoring to design features that drive user engagement and frequent use. By strategically setting reference points within the user experience, they can influence user behavior and perceptions, increasing the adoption and usage of specific features. Consider a fitness app where the product manager sets a recommended weekly workout goal of four sessions. This anchor motivates users to see four workouts as a baseline, encouraging consistent use of the app.

Here are examples of anchoring strategies across various industries:

Product Context	Anchoring Strategy	Example Statement
Task Management App	Anchor with Daily Task Limit	"Complete 5 tasks today."
E-Learning Platform	Course Completion Anchor	"Most users complete this course in 3 weeks."
Financial Planning App	Savings Goal Anchor	"Save $200 per month."
Social Media Platform	Post Frequency Anchor	"Top creators post 3 times per week."
Streaming Service	Watch Time Anchor	"Most users with similar tastes watch 10 hours per week."
E-commerce Platform	Cart Size Anchor	"Customers typically spend $50 per order."
Language Learning App	Daily Practice Anchor	"Practice for 15 minutes a day."
Health and Wellness App	Step Count Anchor	"Most users take 10,000 steps a day."
Travel Booking Platform	Booking Time Anchor	"Most users book 3 months ahead."

Real-World Examples

1. **Zomato and Blinkit:** These platforms use counter-intuitive strategies to anchor users' attention by offering additional discounts for adding more items to the cart, ultimately encouraging higher spending.

2. **Coursera:** Sets completion anchors for courses, motivating users to finish within a suggested time frame.

3. **IndMoney:** Uses small SIP anchors (as low as Rs. 100) to encourage first-time investors to start saving.

4. **Flight Pricing:** A common belief that flight prices are lowest four months before travel has anchored many users' booking decisions.

5. **Retail Sales:** During sales events like Black Friday, retailers often display the original price alongside the discounted price. The original price acts as an anchor, making the discount appear more substantial.

The power of anchoring lies in the way our brains process information. Once an anchor is established, it becomes a mental shortcut that simplifies decision-making. However, this shortcut often prevents individuals from fully analyzing all available information, leading to cognitive biases.

If anchoring is such a powerful tool, how can you counter it as a product manager or business leader? The answer lies in creating a competing anchor combined with a compelling value proposition.

For example, consider a situation where a competitor's product has set a price anchor:

- **Competitor's Anchor:** The user sees the competitor's coffee priced at Rs. 280.

- **Your Product Message:** "Freshly brewed premium coffee at Rs. 380. Not just another coffee."

This message doesn't just address the price anchor but also differentiates your product by highlighting its premium quality. By establishing a new anchor and offering a clear value proposition, you can effectively shift the user's perception and decision-making process.

Practical Tips for Using Anchoring Effectively

1. **Set Strategic Anchors Early:** Introduce the anchor at the beginning of the user journey, such as during onboarding or the first interaction.

2. **Reinforce the Anchor:** Use consistent messaging across touchpoints to solidify the anchor in the user's mind.

3. **Combine Anchors with Social Proof:** Highlight what other users are doing to make the anchor more persuasive.

4. **Monitor and Adjust Anchors:** Regularly evaluate the effectiveness of your anchors and modify them based on user feedback and behavior.

While anchoring can drive business growth, it's essential to use this tool responsibly. Misleading anchors or manipulative practices can harm user trust and long-term brand reputation. Always ensure that the anchors you set align with genuine value propositions and user interests.

Anchoring is a double-edged sword—it can influence users' decisions both positively and negatively. As a product manager, understanding how to use this tool effectively, while being mindful of its potential drawbacks, can make a significant difference in user engagement and business outcomes.

Chapter 21.
Regression to the Mean

Regression to the mean can be simply explained as an extreme outcome followed by a typical outcome. For instance, the initial traction for a product or a campaign might make you believe that you have hit the jackpot, but this could be an illusion of success. If an athlete performs exceptionally well one day, it is likely due to both their skill and some favorable random factors. During their next performance, those random factors may not recur, leading to results closer to their average. This does not indicate a decline in skill but rather the natural variability of random influences.

At TravClan, we have experienced many sales campaigns starting with absolute highs on day one, only to see performance stabilize to average levels over the next two to three days. This pattern occurs because most customers influenced by sales make their purchases early on, leading to lower performance in subsequent days. Additionally, numerous random and unknown factors might contribute to the performance reverting to the mean.

Organizations that incentivize employees for good performance cannot expect consistent high returns every day. Productivity will naturally fluctuate, with periods of high and low performance. Over time, performance regresses to the mean, even with ongoing incentives. Business leaders and managers must understand that such patterns are not indicative of effort levels. Rewards or punishments contribute minimally to overall long-term performance.

Suppose a product team launches a new feature, such as a gamified reward system, to a subset of users and observes a significant spike in engagement. Initially, the spike might result from the novelty of the feature and a highly engaged subset of users. Over time, engagement may regress to the mean as the initial excitement fades. To sustain engagement, the team should focus on long-term metrics and iterate on the feature to maintain user interest.

Let's take another example where a company introduces a referral program, resulting in a surge of new user sign-ups. This initial growth might be driven by early adopters. However, as the program reaches a broader audience, the growth rate could decline and regress to a more typical level. The team must avoid interpreting early success as a permanent trend and continue optimizing the program for sustained growth.

Lowering subscription prices can lead to a sharp increase in sign-ups, often driven by price-sensitive customers. Over time, as this customer segment is exhausted, sign-ups may regress to the mean. The pricing team should avoid making long-term decisions based solely on short-term data and continuously refine pricing strategies.

Similarly, a sales team might achieve an unusually high number of deals in a single month due to favorable market conditions or luck. Future performance is likely to regress to the average. Management should set targets based on long-term trends rather than outlier performance.

More examples in the context of pirate metrics in product management.

Metric	Feature Example	Scenario	Regression to the Mean Insight	Actionable Insight
Acquisition	Free Trial	Launch a 14-day free trial to attract	Initial sign-up spikes may decline	Monitor sign-up trends over several months

		new users.	over time as early excitement fades.	to understand true impact.
Activation	Guided Onboarding	Create an interactive onboarding that helps users complete key tasks.	High completion rates may decrease as users grow accustomed to it.	Continuously improve onboarding to maintain engagement and success.
Retention	Personalized Content Recommendations	Offer suggestions based on user preferences.	Engagement might drop after the novelty wears off.	Regularly refine recommendations to match users' changing interests.
Referral	Social Sharing Incentives	Reward users with discounts or credits for referrals.	Referral spikes may regress as interest in the offer diminishes.	Evaluate long-term incentive effects and adjust rewards accordingly.

| Revenue | Dynamic Pricing | Adjust prices based on behavior or market demand. | Early revenue increases may stabilize as the market adapts. | Continuously test and refine pricing to ensure sustained growth. |

Understanding regression to the mean helps product managers and business leaders avoid overreacting to short-term fluctuations, ensuring decisions are based on sustainable trends rather than temporary spikes. By recognizing this concept, teams can:

- **Focus on Long-Term Metrics:** Avoid over-optimizing for short-term results by tracking metrics over extended periods.

- **Iterate and Optimize Continuously:** Use insights from regressed outcomes to refine strategies and features.

- **Set Realistic Expectations:** Base targets and goals on average performance and long-term trends rather than outliers.

By keeping these principles in mind, businesses can make informed decisions that account for natural fluctuations and sustain growth over time.

Chapter 22.
Cognitive Load

Cognitive Load Theory is a concept that helps us understand how our brains process information. Imagine your brain as a computer with limited memory. When too much information is presented at once, the computer slows down, and tasks become harder to complete. This is similar to what happens when a product or task is too complex for the brain to handle efficiently. Cognitive Load Theory explains how to design products in a way that makes them easier for users to understand and use.

There are three types of cognitive load that product managers should be aware of: intrinsic load, extraneous load, and germane load. Intrinsic load refers to the natural difficulty of a task. For example, learning how to solve a math problem is harder than learning how to add numbers, so it has a higher intrinsic load. In product management, this means that complicated tasks should be broken down into smaller, easier steps to help users understand them better.

Extraneous load, on the other hand, comes from how information is presented to the user. If a product is cluttered with too many buttons or confusing instructions, it can overwhelm the user and make the task harder to complete. As a product manager, you can reduce extraneous load by simplifying the design of your product. This might mean using clear and straightforward language, organizing information logically, or removing unnecessary elements that distract the user.

Germane load is the mental effort that contributes to learning. When users put effort into understanding a product and building mental models, they are experiencing germane load. For product managers, this means creating features that help users learn and remember how to use the product. For example, offering tutorials or practice exercises can enhance germane load by helping users become more familiar with the product.

In product management, understanding cognitive load is crucial for creating user-friendly designs. If a product imposes too much cognitive load, users may become frustrated and abandon it. On the other hand, a well-designed product that minimizes unnecessary cognitive load can improve user satisfaction and keep users engaged.

To reduce cognitive load, product managers can follow a few key principles. First, it's important to minimize unnecessary information. For example, a clean and simple interface that only shows essential actions can help users focus on what really matters. Second, organizing information logically is important. Users should be able to find what they need easily, without getting lost in confusing menus or layouts.

Another important principle is using visual hierarchy. This means making the most important elements stand out by using size, color, or spacing. For example, a "Buy Now" button could be made larger and more colorful to draw the user's attention. Progressive disclosure is another technique that can help reduce cognitive load. This involves only showing users the information they need at the moment, with additional details available if needed.

Finally, providing clear instructions and feedback is essential. Users should always know what actions they need to take and what the results of those actions will be. For example, a form that shows error messages in real-time helps users correct mistakes immediately, reducing confusion and frustration.

Let's look at some examples of how these principles can be applied in product management. One example is a simplified onboarding process that introduces new users to a product's features one at a time, rather than all at once. This makes the learning process easier by reducing the intrinsic load. Another example is using progressive disclosure in a settings menu, where advanced options are hidden until the user needs them. This prevents users from feeling overwhelmed by too many choices.

Visual hierarchy can be used on a landing page by making the primary call-to-action button stand out. This helps users focus on the most important action, reducing the effort needed to navigate the page. Task automation is another way to reduce cognitive load. For instance, a form that auto-fills common information like name and address can save users time and mental effort.

Interactive tutorials are a great way to enhance germane load. By allowing users to practice using a new feature in a safe, simulated environment, they can build confidence and understanding without feeling pressured. This kind of hands-on learning helps users form mental models that make the product easier to use in the future.

Below are some product examples:

Cognitive Load Principle	Product	Example	Explanation
Minimize Unnecessary Information	Google Search	Simplified Search Interface	Google's homepage is minimalist, showing only the search bar and logo, reducing cognitive load by focusing users on the main task.
	Spotify	Home Screen with Suggested Playlists	Spotify's home screen presents a few personalized playlists, keeping the interface clean and reducing unnecessary choices.

	Apple iPhone Settings	Streamlined Settings Menu	Apple organizes settings into clear, labeled categories, avoiding overwhelming users with too many options at once.
Organize Information Logically	Microsoft Word	Ribbon Interface	Microsoft Word uses the Ribbon interface to group related tools together, making it easier for users to find what they need.
	Airbnb	Navigation Tabs	Airbnb organizes its app into tabs like "Explore," "Wishlists," and "Profile," helping users quickly access different sections.
	LinkedIn	Profile Setup Progress Bar	LinkedIn uses a step-by-step profile setup process, guiding users logically through each section to complete their profiles.
Use Visual Hierarchy	Amazon	"Buy Now" Button	Amazon's "Buy Now" button is prominently placed and stands out, directing the user's

			attention to the key action.
	Netflix	Featured Content Carousel	Netflix highlights its featured shows with large images and bold titles, making it easy for users to decide what to watch.
	Medium	Article Layout	Medium uses large, bold headlines and clear spacing to guide readers through an article, highlighting important information.
Progressive Disclosure	Facebook	Advanced Privacy Settings	Facebook hides advanced privacy options under expandable sections, showing basic settings first to reduce overwhelm.
	Google Maps	Layer Options	Google Maps initially shows the basic map view, with additional layers like traffic and satellite view hidden until needed.

	Slack	Notification Preferences	Slack presents basic notification settings upfront, with advanced customization options available under an expandable menu.
Clear Instructions and Feedback	Trello	Real-time Card Updates	Trello provides immediate visual feedback when tasks are moved or updated, helping users understand the impact of their actions.
	Gmail	Error Messages for Emails	Gmail displays clear, real-time error messages if there's an issue with sending an email, guiding users to correct the problem.
	Duolingo	Language Learning Progress	Duolingo gives instant feedback on answers, using green for correct and red for incorrect, helping users learn and adjust quickly.

Cognitive Load Theory is an essential tool for product managers who want to create intuitive and user-friendly products. By understanding and managing the different types of cognitive load, you can design products that are easier to use, more enjoyable, and more likely to keep users coming back.

Chapter 23.
Causes Triumphs Statistics

As a product manager, convincing stakeholders to align on a problem often requires more than just presenting raw data—it demands a narrative that connects the data to real user impact. Our minds are wired to seek causes behind outcomes, and stories anchored in user experiences often carry more weight than standalone statistics. While it's worthwhile to use such causes to gather support, knowing how to make decisions when faced with statistical information is crucial for ensuring product success. Striking the right balance between emotion-driven narratives and data-backed reasoning is an essential skill for every product manager.

Our minds are hungry for searching for causes to explain the story. Any statistical fact that supports the outcome is usually included in decision making whereas if the statistics do not directly relate to cause it is often ignored in decision making. Below are some examples of statistical statements as well as the causal statements.

1. Fitness App - Workout Personalization

- Base Statement: "Users who engage with our workout personalization feature have a 5% higher frequency of app use compared to those who don't."

- Causal Statement: "Sophie reported that with personalized workout plans, she increased her workout frequency by 20% and achieved her fitness goals 30% faster."

2. E-Commerce Platform - Product Recommendations

- Base Statement: "Product recommendations increase average order value by 7% based on user purchase history."

- Causal Statement: "John found that personalized recommendations led to a 15% increase in his total purchases and discovered 3 new products he now regularly buys."

3. Music Streaming Service - Playlist Curation

    - Base Statement: "Users who use curated playlists spend 10% more time listening to music than those who create their own playlists."

    - Causal Statement: "Emily's use of curated playlists resulted in a 25% increase in her listening time, and she discovered 5 new favorite artists through these playlists."

4. Social Media App - Content Filtering

    - Base Statement: "Content filtering features reduce the time users spend on irrelevant content by 15%."

    - Causal Statement: "David experienced a 20% reduction in time spent on irrelevant posts and reported a 30% increase in meaningful interactions due to content filtering."

5. Online Learning Platform - Progress Tracking

    - Base Statement: "Users who regularly check their progress are 8% more likely to complete their courses."

    - Causal Statement: "Laura, who checked her progress weekly, increased her course completion rate by 25% and completed her courses 40% faster than average users."

6. Travel Booking Site - Trip Recommendations

    - Base Statement: "Trip recommendations lead to a 6% increase in booking conversions compared to users who browse without recommendations."

- Causal Statement: "Tom, using personalized trip recommendations, booked his trip 35% faster and showed a 20% higher satisfaction rate compared to standard browsing."

7. Health App - Daily Reminders

- Base Statement: "Daily reminders for medication adherence increase usage rates by 4%."

- Causal Statement: "Alice saw a 50% improvement in her medication adherence rate, leading to a significant 40% improvement in her overall health management."

8. Project Management Tool - Task Prioritization

- Base Statement: "Task prioritization features have shown a 5% increase in project completion rates."

- Causal Statement: "Michael's use of task prioritization led to a 30% faster project completion rate and a 20% increase in team productivity."

9. Financial Management App - Budget Alerts

- Base Statement: "Budget alerts reduce overspending by 3% compared to users who do not use them."

- Causal Statement: "Nina reported a 15% decrease in overspending and saved an additional $200 per month due to the effective budget alerts."

10. Customer Support Platform - Automated Responses

- Base Statement: "Automated responses resolve 12% of customer inquiries faster than manual responses."

- Causal Statement: "Mark experienced a 25% reduction in resolution time for his inquiries and reported a 30% increase in satisfaction with automated responses."

Incorporating causal narratives can be a powerful tool to inspire action and gain stakeholder buy-in. However, as a product manager, your ultimate success lies in your ability to critically assess statistical information and decide based on a holistic view of the data. By marrying stories with facts and carefully analyzing the validity and relevance of the data, you can make decisions that not only resonate with stakeholders but also drive meaningful outcomes for your product and its users.

Chapter 24.
Endowment Effect

My hometown is a small place where life is relatively slow. Unlike big cities where space is a big constraint, small towns are completely different with a lot of spaces. If you visit my town, it is typical to find a store in every other house. A look around the storeroom, and you would find it filled with things not used for years. Why don't they sell it? Many of you would be able to relate to this situation. You have possession of things that have hardly been used over the years. But when the time comes, you find yourself struggling to discard them. You attach enough value to them to perceive them as useful. This is a classic example of the endowment effect, where people assign more value to things simply because they own them. The endowment effect explains why people in my hometown hold onto items they rarely use; the mere ownership increases the perceived value, making it difficult to let go, even if these items no longer serve a practical purpose.

This psychological phenomenon has vast applications in product management and designing products. Product managers can use it to increase engagement, retention, and the overall emotional quotient of a product. One of the most well-known examples of the endowment effect in action comes from the retail giant IKEA. IKEA is famous for its flat-pack furniture that customers assemble themselves. This "IKEA effect," a variation of the endowment effect, highlights how customers place a higher value on furniture they build themselves compared to pre-assembled pieces. The effort and time invested in assembling the furniture create a sense of ownership, making the product feel more valuable. This phenomenon has been a key factor in IKEA's success, as customers feel more connected to the products they have physically worked on, even though the actual monetary value of the item hasn't changed. The endowment effect plays a crucial role here, as the hands-on experience of assembling the furniture creates a personal connection, leading customers to value the product more than if it were pre-assembled.

When users feel ownership of data within an application, the endowment effect is at play. Users who use the applications create a lot of content and ultimately feel ownership of the content and the data generated in the process of using it. This data becomes powerful when it can solve your users' problems. The endowment effect causes users to place more value on the data they have personally generated, increasing their attachment to the application and making them less likely to switch to a competitor.

I have had many health goals over the years – trying swimming, going to the gym, practicing martial arts, and running. One problem that continues to haunt me to this day is staying consistent with my practice. I have never had enough motivation to keep going. I would start going to the gym, and after a couple of weeks, begin questioning its value. Thoughts like, "Why can't I do similar exercises at home?" Would arise, and I would eventually find it boring and stop altogether.

Over the years, I've been using an app called RunKeeper to track my runs. Spurts of motivation come and go, usually lasting only a day or two each week or month. Despite my inconsistency even with running, as time passed, more and more data got fed into the app. Slowly, I started feeling proud of my stats. I now proudly share my progress with my friends whenever we discuss exercise and health goals. I take pride in my first 5k run, my 100th run, my first 10k, and more. After using RunKeeper for many years, I upgraded to the paid version of the app and began training for various programs. My runs are all logged with different statistics: my personal best 5k, my personal best 10k, my longest run, and many other stats. This data has brought me back to running multiple times after months of hiatus. It's like having a permanent resume that will stick with me forever. Data can create stickiness by generating emotional value over time.

The endowment effect keeps me renewing the membership every year. In return, the app pushes me to do better every time. Here, the endowment effect is evident as the accumulation of data over time makes the app more valuable to me, enhancing my emotional connection and leading to continued engagement and subscription renewal.

Another interesting example can be found in a food ordering app. Customers order from various places and often forget the names of the outlets where they enjoyed a delicious meal. Features like 'recently ordered' and 'order again' are prime examples of using data to bring users back to the app. Imagine two friends chatting on a Friday evening. The user journey leading to a repeat order might look like this: "That place had some great sandwiches." "What was the name of the place?" "Let me check the name on the app." "Open the online store." "End up browsing the whole menu." "Craving for the sandwich increases." "Let's order again." The value of data and the convenience of repeat ordering result in another sale in this case. The endowment effect here is subtle but significant; the ease of access to past orders and the emotional connection to previous positive experiences increase the likelihood of a repeat purchase, as users feel a sense of ownership over their past choices.

Booking a flight is not a simple task. Numerous considerations come to mind for a traveler: Are flight seats comfortable? Does the price fit my budget? Will I get preferred meal options? Do the flight timings suit my itinerary? What if I need to cancel or reschedule? Will the price increase if I don't book today? Let's examine the user actions involved in booking a flight ticket: Visit website 1 Log into the website Search for flights with the desired schedule (day and time) Look for the correct price point Enter personal details Check the cancellation policy Review baggage information See the final price with tax

This same process repeats for website 1, website 2, website 3, and so on. A close analysis of customer behavior reveals that they search for various flights and often abandon the process at the payment page once they know the final price. Users juggle through multiple websites and input travelers' information. To increase booking success, the product should streamline this process. Saving user information and preserving search history are examples that can help convert more customers. These features enable auto-filling customer details or even resuming a booking, reducing customer cognitive load and drop-offs from the funnel. The endowment effect is at play here as well; by saving user information and previous searches, the product increases the perceived value of the platform, making users more likely to complete the booking and less likely to switch to another site.

All learning applications face a common challenge – maintaining consistent learner engagement. Users often drop off after a few sessions or days. Numerous edtech companies have attempted to solve this problem. I have been using Coursera for some time. Over the years, Coursera's interface has evolved to address issues related to learner motivation, consistency, and course completion rates. They have incorporated hyper-personalization into their product to enhance learner consistency and motivation. When you log into the platform, it prompts you to set your own goals. It then guides you in creating a personalized schedule, motivates you to complete courses, displays your course progress, and encourages you to stay on track. The endowment effect is utilized here by allowing learners to set personalized goals and track their progress, creating a sense of ownership over their educational journey and making them more committed to completing courses.

If you closely observe, the common thread in all these examples is that all the data is generated by the user. It's something the user creates as part of their activities. It's information specific to that particular user. While many applications use this personalized information for marketing and business purposes, the true power for a product manager lies in becoming a data wizard – utilizing this information to fulfill users' goals, ultimately enhancing renewal and retention metrics. A skilled product person understands that this personalized information is a treasure trove on which adoption-focused features can be seamlessly built. The endowment effect amplifies this by increasing the user's perceived value of their data and personalized experiences, leading to stronger attachment and lower churn rates.

Products that store user information have less churn compared to other products. By allowing users to personalize or customize their experience, they become more attached to the product, increasing their loyalty, and reducing the likelihood of churn. This is a direct application of the endowment effect, where personalization and customization foster a sense of ownership, making users less willing to abandon the product.

More examples from the product world:

- **Customizable Dashboards:** Allowing users to personalize their dashboard layout or widget settings, fostering a sense of ownership. The endowment effect makes users more likely to stay with the product because they have invested time in making it their own.

- **Profile Customization:** Enabling users to upload avatars, set preferences, and personalize their profiles, making them more invested in the product. The endowment effect strengthens their connection to the platform, reducing the chance of churn.

- **Saved Preferences:** Offering users the ability to save their settings or preferences for future use, reinforcing their connection to the product. The endowment effect plays a role in making users feel that the product is tailored to their needs, increasing retention.

- **Personalized Content Feeds:** Providing a tailored content feed based on user behavior, which makes users feel that the product is uniquely theirs. The endowment effect makes these personalized feeds more valuable, enhancing user satisfaction and loyalty.

- **Gamification Elements:** Allowing users to earn badges, achievements, or points that reflect their engagement and create a sense of accomplishment and ownership. The endowment effect makes these rewards more meaningful, encouraging continued use of the product.

Chapter 25.
Prospects Theory: Decision Under Risk

I find the concept of Prospect Theory - how people make decisions under uncertainty and risk, often deviating from rational economic behavior. Instead of evaluating final outcomes logically, people assess potential gains and losses relative to a reference point -to be the most impactful in understanding how people make decisions under uncertainty and risk. For business and product applications, it has wide-ranging implications. Understanding how customers choose to use a product, what price points they find risky, or what they perceive as significant rewards is vital for business success. Traditional economic theories assume people always make rational choices to maximize benefit, but Prospect Theory suggests that people often think about possible gains and losses in ways that aren't entirely logical. One important idea in Prospect Theory is the "reference point." This is the situation a person compares everything else to when deciding.

At TravClan, we designed a scratch card system that travel agents received after each booking. This was the initial pitch the onboarding sales team used to get them to transact for the first time. While it might seem obsolete, a small travel agent who completes fewer bookings may see this as an opportunity to earn more because their reference point is their own earnings. A scratch card that offers Rs. 50 or Rs. 100 adds value to their current business. However, the same scratch card value might not be lucrative for high-earning agents. Consider the following agent profiles:

Agent A: Completes 10 daily bookings, earning Rs. 100 on each booking
Agent B: Completes 100 daily bookings, earning Rs. 100 on each booking
Agent C: Completes 500 daily bookings, earning Rs. 100 on each booking

What value of scratch cards will each of them find appealing?

For Agent A, who completes 10 daily bookings, the Rs. 50 or Rs. 100 from the scratch card is a significant addition to their earnings, making it an attractive incentive. This aligns with Prospect Theory, where individuals assess potential gains or losses relative to a personal reference point—in this case, their regular earnings. Agent B, with 100 daily bookings, might see the scratch card as a smaller but still notable benefit. However, for Agent C, who handles 500 daily bookings, the same reward may seem negligible and might not motivate them as much. Their reference point is much higher, so the perceived value of the reward diminishes.

If I were to design a scratch card system based on Prospect Theory, it could not be the same for all users. The system's rules would need to consider the agent's business size to maintain high utility for each customer segment. Moreover, as agents' businesses grow and they move from Category A to Category B and C, they should experience increased marginal utility over time.

Many companies, such as Paytm, don't reward customers with monetary benefits but prefer to offer gift vouchers to keep users engaged. The definition of value changes based on the type of voucher a user receives. One user might prefer a shopping voucher, while another might prefer movie tickets. If I prefer movies over shopping, I won't see value in Paytm's reward system if I consistently receive shopping vouchers. As a result, it's highly likely I would shift to competitors over time.

How do companies solve this particular problem? Rewarding customers based on their preferences is one way, but collecting relevant data might be challenging. However, once done successfully, this becomes a powerful tool for customer retention.

Let's look at another example—memberships. When you pay for a membership, you're essentially betting on how much you'll use it. This is where uncertainty comes in. Let's explore three different types of memberships: Zomato Pro, holiday memberships, and gym memberships.

Food Memberships (like Zomato and Swiggy): Companies often offer a three-month membership at a discounted price of Rs. 149. If you order food online regularly, this membership might seem like a great deal. You could save money on delivery fees and get discounts on meals. But what if you're not sure how often you'll order food in the next three months? If you only end up ordering a few times, the Rs. 149 might feel like a waste. The value of the membership depends on your confidence in how much you'll use it. Users have reference points, such as the number of times they recently ordered or specific events like an upcoming birthday, which increases the likelihood of usage. Companies use past data, such as ordering behavior and user information like dates of birth, to time and price memberships effectively, making them look attractive to customers. Some users might get the membership at Rs. 99, while others pay Rs. 149, often receiving prompts around their birthdays.

Holiday Memberships: Vacation memberships can be quite expensive. However, if you're someone who plans holidays every year, this membership might be a good investment. You'll have access to great vacation spots and probably save money over time. But if you're unsure how often you'll take vacations, the high cost of the membership could seem too risky. The uncertainty of whether you'll use it enough makes the decision harder. For instance, if you're already on vacation and a company offers you a membership, you're more likely to buy it because your current vacation creates a reference point, making future vacations feel more probable.

Gym Memberships: Gym memberships are another example where usage plays a big role. If you're committed to working out regularly, a gym membership offers great value. You get access to equipment, classes, and a space dedicated to fitness. But if you're unsure how often you'll go to the gym, the membership might not seem like such a good deal. Paying for something you might not use often feels risky, leading you to possibly opt out because of that uncertainty.

As a product manager designing products or strategies like scratch cards or memberships, it's important to think about your customers' habits and expectations. For a travel agent with a small business, a Rs. 50 scratch cards can be valuable. For someone who orders food often, the Zomato membership could save a lot of money. But if customers are unsure about how often they'll use a service, the offers might not be worth it.

Prospect Theory helps us understand these choices. People don't just look at the possible outcomes; they think about how those outcomes compare to their current situation. A small reward might feel significant to someone with limited means, while a large cost might feel too risky to someone unsure about their usage. By considering these factors, businesses can design better products and offers that meet their customers' needs and expectations.

Understanding these concepts can help product managers and businesses create more effective strategies that appeal to different types of customers. Whether it's offering a small reward to encourage more bookings or creating a membership plan that feels like a great deal, knowing how people make decisions under uncertainty is key to success.

Part IV.
Experimentation

One of the most important tasks of a product manager is to solve customer problems. It might seem obvious but often the business is engaged in solving irrelevant problems on a day-to-day basis. Many entrepreneurs and product managers often fall into the trap of building ideas mostly on hunches, shiny presentations or merely how good the numbers look on papers. These can result in costly business mistakes. Testing business ideas helps in reducing the risk on costly ventures. But a more preceding step is to find the right problem to solve. How do you know whether the problem that you are trying to solve is actually the one that your customer values? Moreover, how do you know that the problem makes business sense? There are various discovery techniques that help you find the right problem to focus upon. Overall, the product managers focus on three objectives:

1. Finding the right Problems
2. Finding the right solution
3. Validating the solution: Testing - Desirability. Feasibility. Viability

The next set of chapters focus on how product managers can effectively achieve each of the objectives.

Chapter 26.
Customer Support Tickets

One of the hardest things for any product team is deciding which problem to solve first. Without clear data, it's just a guessing game. Support tickets provide exactly that—quantifiable data that can guide decision-making. When you categorize and count tickets by product and issue type, you get a clear picture of where the most significant pain points are.

Support tickets are more than just records of complaints or issues—they are a gold mine of insights. Each ticket tells a story of friction, miscommunication, or a flaw in the process. When systematically tracked and analyzed, these tickets can uncover patterns that help teams identify the most impactful problems to solve.

When we started setting up the customer experience function at TravClan, we didn't know what to do. The team was relatively young, with little experience in understanding what customer experience truly entails. Initially, customer experience was synonymous with solving escalations. Moreover, there was no measurable way to identify which problems had the most significant impact. We began by tracking everything.

We set up an escalation support number, and the team manually listened to and logged the calls. Each email sent to the escalation inbox was recorded, and an internal system was established for employees to raise issues. These issues were categorized by product and issue type. For example, if there was an escalation for a hotels product, it was tagged under the "Refund" category if it was related to reimbursement. This process made everything measurable, and for the first time, we had a way to prioritize issues based on their frequency and severity. The data revealed that refund-related issues were a significant pain point across different products. We improved several processes, and some key features were built, eventually leading to faster, automated refunds.

Refund complaints were initially seen as individual incidents. However, as the tickets piled up, we recognized a recurring theme. The refund process was not just slow but inconsistent across products, leading to frustration and escalation. By digging deeper into these complaints, we identified three key areas for improvement: the automation of refunds wherever possible, communication gaps with customers, and discrepancies in refund timelines for different products. The solution wasn't just about fixing a specific case; it required rethinking the entire process and building an improved process across the board.

Support tickets are the voice of the customer. When users encounter problems, they reach out to support teams, articulating their frustrations and challenges. By reviewing these tickets, product managers can identify common themes and recurring problems. This allows product managers to take a user-centric approach, focusing on real-world challenges rather than assumptions about what users want.

For example, if multiple tickets report issues with a specific feature (like a search function), this indicates a tangible problem that affects the user experience. Even when data analytics show that users are engaging with a feature, support tickets reveal the qualitative side of the story—how they are feeling and what they expect.

Most companies fail to utilize support tickets effectively. These are often not organized in a manner that can be tracked, and hence they miss out on opportunities lying wide open. Doing this on an ongoing basis is an even bigger challenge for organizations.

How to Leverage Support Tickets

1. **Create Channels for Customers to Reach Out:** It can be a simple email or a "Contact Us" form.

2. **Set Up Systems for Categorization:** Use tags or categories to group support tickets based on issue type, urgency, and impact. This allows easier pattern recognition.

3. **Collaborate with Support Teams:** Build a close working relationship with the support team to ensure they can quickly escalate critical issues. This is especially important in large organizations.

4. **Track KPIs:** Measure key performance indicators (KPIs) related to support tickets, such as ticket resolution time and the number of tickets associated with particular features and severity.

5. **Use Feedback in Roadmaps:** Actively incorporate insights from support tickets into product roadmaps. Make sure customers feel heard by addressing their concerns in product releases.

Chapter 27.
Launch a Training Programme

Many companies have structured training programs. These programs are traditionally designed to educate users about a product's features and functionalities. However, these programs not only help your customers but also provide valuable feedback that can guide product managers what to build next. By increasing product proficiency, customers can maximize the value they derive from the product. On the other hand, interactions during training sessions provide firsthand insights into user challenges, feature requests, and usage patterns to product managers.

One way this is different from customer interviews is the comfort at which customers share feedback without any obligation. In customer interviews, users are usually aware that their responses are being analyzed so they either end up giving feedback or it is highly directed by the interviewee which might lead to certain types of bias. Whereas in customer training, users usually end up talking about their problems.

Training sessions create an open environment where customers feel comfortable sharing their experiences. Product managers can gather direct feedback on:

- **Usability Issues**: Identifying features that are difficult to use or understand.
- **Feature Requests**: Learning what additional functionalities customers desire.
- **Pain Points**: Understanding problems that hinder customer satisfaction.

Moreover, live training allows product managers to observe how customers interact with the product in real-time, revealing: areas where users frequently err, indicating design flaws. You can also observe for features with least or most utilized. A feature which has most questions or is difficult to grasp usually indicates a large learning curve or lower usability for example, if trainees constantly struggle with a particular feature, it may prompt a redesign to improve intuitiveness.

There are additional benefits of training programs for product managers that set the stage for future discovery. Training programs strengthen relationships with customers, fostering loyalty and open communication. Engaged customers are more likely to participate in Beta Testing providing early feedback on new features and advocate for the Product promoting it within their networks. For example, a customer who feels supported through training may volunteer for user interviews or case studies, offering deeper insights into their needs.

Aggregating feedback from multiple training sessions can help identify broader market trends, competition, and common needs across the customer base. Our training session at TravClan was designed in a way that sufficient time is dedicated to discussion where customers could ask questions. These have resulted in some of the biggest insights where we would not look in our routine. There was some obvious feedback which was neglected due to incorrect prioritization. We ensured that the training happened in a group of 10 customers. This ensured that everyone had the opportunity to interact and also it was never overcrowded and uncontrolled. It is usually not a hard number. Sometimes the group tends to be smaller with 5-6 people and larger with 10 people. But usually, the most effective training happens in a batch of 8-15 customers. All sessions were structured in the following way:

1. 5 mins: Explain that the session is a small group. And it is planned to be interactive so that customers can get maximum value out of it.

2. 2 mins: Explain to participants what will be covered so that they have a broader idea about how it will pan out.

3. 2 min: explain that we would want to avoid discussing any existing or ongoing complaints or escalation. We can connect separately for those discussions. This was done to ensure that the session objective remains on track.

4. 25-30 mins: Interactive training

5. 15 mins: Feedback discussion

These sessions have helped us learn a lot more about the customers than any other method. Good thing is that customers volunteer to be part of the discussion rather than force. You also get a broader perspective rather than being influenced by a single view point.

It might seem a routine task but it is one of the best practices for the product manager to attend these training sessions. In order to get the maximum result, you should conduct and facilitate the same. This is what you should do:

1. Collaborate with Training Teams

   a. Align Objectives: Work with trainers to identify key areas where feedback is needed.

   b. Share Insights: Provide trainers with information on upcoming features to gauge customer interest.

2. Engage Actively in Training Programs

   a. Attend Sessions: Participate in training to hear customer feedback firsthand.

   b. Facilitate Discussions: Encourage questions and open dialogue to uncover deeper insights.

3. Utilize Training Data

   a. Analyze Feedback: Collect and review feedback forms, surveys, and discussion points.

b. Identify Patterns: Look for recurring themes or issues that could inform product decisions.

4. Foster Continuous Learning Communities

   a. Online Forums: Create platforms where customers can continue discussions post-training.

   b. Follow-Up Sessions: Schedule additional training or webinars to delve deeper into complex topics.

Organizing training programs for customers offers a strategic advantage for product managers. These programs not only empower users but also serve as a rich source of information on how customers interact with the product, what challenges they face, and what features they desire. By actively engaging with customers during training, product managers can make informed decisions about product enhancements, new feature development, and overall strategy. But one of the core challenges that organizations face is being able to do this regularly.

Here is how you can integrate this your work:

- Integrate Training into Product Strategy: Make customer training a core component of product development processes.

- Allocate Resources: Invest in skilled trainers and robust training platforms that facilitate feedback collection.

- Measure Impact: Establish metrics to assess how training influences product improvements and customer satisfaction.

- Stay Responsive: Act on the feedback received promptly to show customers that their input is valued.

By embracing customer training programs as a feedback mechanism, product managers can better align their products with customer needs, leading to increased adoption, loyalty, and success in the marketplace.

Chapter 28.
Surveys

Surveys are one of the most powerful tools in a product manager's toolkit to work at scale. They allow you to gain direct insights from users, validate assumptions, and make data-driven decisions. Unlike anecdotal feedback or educated guesses, surveys offer structured data that helps product managers understand user needs, uncover pain points, and prioritize features. When designed carefully surveys help you focus on solving the right problems in product development. In this chapter, we will explore the practical aspects of using surveys, from designing them to leveraging them for growth.

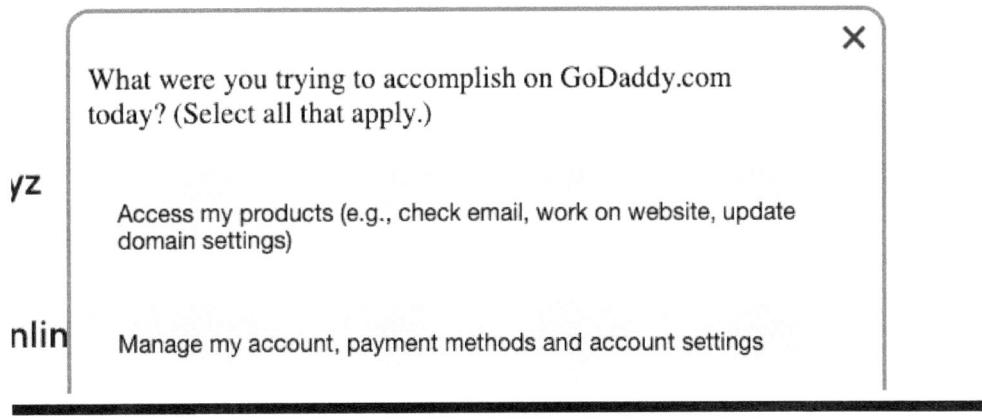

GoDaddy using surveys

Before diving into design, product managers should ask: What do I want to learn? Whether it's identifying user frustrations, validating a feature idea, or measuring the success of an update, having a clear goal guides the entire process. Without this focus, surveys can become unfocused, leading to irrelevant data, and wasted effort. Therefore, it's crucial to write down a concise objective before drafting questions to ensure they align with the answers we seek.

Once the objective is clear, it's essential you target the right audience. Survey responses are only valuable if they come from users who can provide meaningful feedback. For instance, if you're trying to prioritize features for power users, surveying new or inactive users won't yield actionable insights. Segment your audience based on behavior, product usage, or demographics. For example, if you are interested in understanding why users drop off after onboarding, focus on respondents who didn't make it past that stage. The more targeted your audience, the more relevant and specific your data will be. Tools like Amplitude and Clevertap are useful to find targeted users.

Survey design is where many product managers struggle. Once you start crafting questions you will find that it is not straight forward. You might end up asking a completely different question than the one you wanted the answers to. You need to ensure that questions are both simple. Start with closed-ended questions that provide quantifiable data, such as ratings or multiple-choice options. These are particularly useful when you need a quick understanding of users' sentiment. However, open-ended questions should not be ignored, as they can reveal unexpected insights. Asking users, what do you find most frustrating about this feature? allows them to explain in their own words, often providing details that quantitative data alone might miss. This is also a source of user innovation. One key rule of thumb is to avoid leading questions — these can bias responses and skew your results, leading to decisions based on inaccurate data. For example, instead of asking, do you agree that our product is easy to use? ask, how easy or difficult do you find our product to use?

Another important aspect of survey design is keeping it short and focused. Users are more likely to complete a survey if it doesn't feel like a chore. A survey that includes only essential questions is more likely to yield better completion rates. Aim for 2 to 3 questions, prioritizing the ones that will deliver the most actionable insights. One question is best. Once you have designed your survey, it's essential to test it with a small group before sending it to a broader audience. This helps you catch any unclear wording or technical glitches that could compromise the results.

Different types of surveys serve different purposes. For example, feature prioritization surveys help you understand what users value most. If you are considering multiple new features, asking users to rank them in order of importance helps focus your development efforts on the right areas. Customer satisfaction surveys (CSAT) are a great way to gauge how happy users are with your product. A simple question like, how satisfied are you with your experience using our product? can reveal whether users are having a positive experience or if there are underlying issues. Similarly, Net Promoter Score (NPS) surveys measure customer loyalty by asking, how likely are you to recommend this product to a friend or colleague? A low NPS score could indicate a significant problem, such as poor user experience or unmet expectations that requires further investigation. For usability testing, usability surveys provide insights into how easy or difficult it is for users to complete specific tasks, helping you pinpoint where users encounter friction in your product. I personally believe a follow up call to some percentage of the users is the most effective way to understand their response.

We have used this strategy time and again at TravClan. We created a platform to create packages for the travel agent. But there was a significant drop from search to final package creation. In order to understand the issue, we introduced an exit intent pop up where we collected the requirements directly. This was followed by a call by the product team to understand why the user did not create the package online and submitted the requirement offline. This activity led to many insights like they cannot find hotels easily; they don't know how to use a recently introduced feature and many more. Now this might seem like a not so scalable solution but it effectively integrates scale with qualitative understanding of the user.

Once you have collected your survey data, the real work lies in analyzing the results and turning them into actionable insights. A simple way to achieve it is to categories and try to map it with the user problem you were trying to solve. For example, if a significant portion of your users report difficulty with the same feature, that's a clear indicator of where to focus your development efforts. Segmenting your data based on user behavior or demographics can also help you uncover more specific insights. For instance, new users might report different pain points than old users, and this segmentation allows you to think of solutions for different groups. In order to ensure these learning is not limited to a product manager we need to build a culture of collective learning and sharing within the organization—share them with marketing, sales, and support teams. This ensures that your entire organization is aligned with the voice of the customer.

Companies like Slack and TravClan have leveraged surveys to drive product growth. Slack's early success was partly due to its iterative feedback loop, in which they conducted regular surveys to understand how teams were using the platform and which features mattered most to them. This user-driven approach helped shape Slack into an indispensable tool for team collaboration. TravClan, on the other hand, continually surveys its user in OnTrip application collecting insights on what is most important for travelers during the trip. This feedback has led to improvements such as safety and food.

Surveys are an invaluable tool for product managers looking to solve the right problems. The beauty of the survey is its clarity of results. They provide direct insights from users, helping you prioritize features, measure satisfaction, and identify pain points. When designed effectively and used consistently, surveys become a critical part of the product development process, ensuring that you're always solving your customers' pain point effectively.

Chapter 29.
Real-Time Interactions

There is no better option to get into the minds of the customer than being able to interact with them while they are using the product. Real-time interactions—whether through calls or live chats - offer a unique and immediate window into the problems of your customers. Unlike data collected through analytics platforms or feedback gathered after a time delay, real-time conversations give product managers the opportunity to experience the full breadth of a user's experience. There are two active ways a product manager can jump on a call with the customers - one as a product manager to take live feedback and second as a sales person trying to make the actual sale. Both of these result in two different types of conversation and insight.

When you jump on a real-time call with a customer as product manager, the immediacy of the conversation allows for deeper insight. Customers are mostly comfortable and less irritated if you ask them for feedback. The real time nature of the conversation helps you get a sense of what's working, what's not, and why the user might be facing certain frustrations. This approach provides real-time insight into user problems that may not be apparent through usage data alone. For instance, at TravClan, we learned through real time calls with travel agents that while creating a holiday package they were searching for hotels, but our system only provided travclan contracted hotels. This gap between user expectations and product functionality became clear in a way that data analysis could have never revealed. The agents were actively looking for a broader range of options, something that was impossible to capture without hearing it directly from them during their daily workflow. These conversations validated the already ongoing plans for integrating online inventory into the holiday flow giving more confidence to the product team.

Similarly, when you connect with customers as sales teams, it results in a different but equally impactful conversation. Salespeople often encounter blockers that prevent users from fully engaging with or purchasing a product. Through such live calls, product managers can identify objections or issues as they arise, whether it's confusion about pricing, uncertainty about product features, or concerns about long-term value. This allows the product manager to address these objections on the spot, helping to remove barriers and clear the path for conversion. These conversations can expose crucial insights, such as the discovery that a key feature is misunderstood, or that potential clients are comparing your offering to a competitor in ways you hadn't considered.

Though both product feedback calls and sales calls are for different purposes, they have an advantage: the ability to address issues as they surface. Product feedback may focus on how the product is used, while sales calls tackle customer objections, but in both cases, real-time calls generate actionable insights that lead to improved product offerings and smoother sales processes.

One of the most important advantages of real-time conversations is that they capture emotions—something that is often lost when feedback is delayed. The emotional state of the user when they are experiencing a problem can be telling. For example, if a user is frustrated with a slow-loading page during a call, the tone in their voice—the rising tension, the pause when they struggle with a task—can convey the depth of their frustration. This allows product managers to connect with the user's experience in a way that data or surveys simply can't replicate. In fact, emotions tend to fade over time, meaning delayed feedback often misses these critical cues. By contrast, real-time calls allow you to seize the moment, capturing the frustration or excitement of a user's experience right when it happens.

Capturing these emotions also helps product managers build trust and empathy with users. When a customer feels heard and understood, they are more likely to engage in future conversations and share honest feedback. This level of openness can transform a transactional relationship into a long-term partnership, where users are invested in the success of the product because they feel their input directly influences its development. This creates a feedback loop where users trust that their voice matters, and product managers can continue to refine the product based on real, human insights.

One of the challenges product managers faces is turning these emotional insights into actionable data. While real-time calls provide valuable qualitative feedback, tools like Amplitude are essential for pairing that with quantitative data. For example, a user may express frustration during a call about a complex feature, but analytics tools like Amplitude can show you exactly how many users are struggling with that same feature. By integrating real-time conversations with data-driven insights, product managers can make more informed decisions, balancing the emotional aspect of user feedback with hard numbers that highlight trends across a broader user base.

These real time conversations can happen both on call as well as chat. You can use tools like Amplitude to see user action streams in real-time to target users for calls. There are many chat products available in the market to help you connect with users in real time. Though it might first feel that chats are not as useful in capturing emotions, you will soon find that a certain set of users are more comfortable expressing in written rather than on call. Moreover, real-time calls and chats allow for adaptability. Realtime conversation enables product managers to uncover insights that might not have been apparent at the beginning of the conversation. In contrast, feedback collected later—whether through surveys or automated tools—tends to be more rigid, often missing the opportunity to explore nuances that arise in the moment.

Real-time conversation - whether conducted as product managers or salespeople—offer a powerful, immediate method of understanding users. As product managers, these calls reveal user pain points in the moment, allowing for faster problem-solving and more empathetic product development. Sales calls help overcome objections and move prospects closer to conversion helping the product people actually understand what customers think before actually making the purchase.

While the objectives may differ, both types of calls lead to better results by capturing the nuances of human interaction that are otherwise lost in delayed feedback. And when combined with analytics tools, these insights become even more valuable, as they create a comprehensive picture of both the emotional and behavioral aspects of user interaction.

Chapter 30.
Customer Interviews

Customer interviews are one of the most effective tools in a product manager's toolkit for uncovering insights about users' needs, challenges, and motivations. They involve direct conversations with current or potential users to understand their experiences, behaviors, and pain points. By engaging in these discussions, product teams can identify the root of user problems and gather inspiration for innovative solutions.

Customer interviews are an excellent way to understand users, but they come with challenges. One common issue is that customers may struggle to explain what they truly need. They might say things like, "I just want it to be easier," without giving details. Another challenge is bias in their answers. Sometimes, customers try to say what they think the interviewer wants to hear instead of being honest. They might avoid giving negative feedback because they don't want to offend anyone.

It can also be hard for customers to remember details about their experiences. When asked about a specific event, they may say, "I can't remember," or mix up the facts. Some customers dominate the conversation, talking about unrelated topics and making it hard to focus on the real problem. On the other hand, some people give very short answers, like "It's fine," and don't provide enough information. This can happen if they feel shy or unsure about what to say.

Another challenge is when customers focus too much on suggesting solutions instead of explaining their problems. For example, they might say, "You should add a button for that," without sharing why they think it's needed. These challenges can make it tricky to gather useful information, but with patience, good questions, and active listening, interviewers can overcome them and uncover valuable insights.

Rajat is a product manager at an early-stage B2B food ordering company, working on one of the key initiatives. He has a strong technical background suited for building complex products. The product is being built for internal users. Like any other rockstar product manager, he starts with the customer. He spends weeks tirelessly talking to them, listening, and building everything according to their requirements. Below is the brief of two conversations between Rajat and the customer.

Rajat's Customer Interview: Correct vs. Incorrect

Conversation A	Conversation B
Rajat: Hi there! Thanks for taking the time to chat with me about our food ordering system. I want to understand your needs better so we can build the perfect solution for you. Can you walk me through your current ordering process?	Rajat: Hi there! Thanks for taking the time to chat with me about our food ordering system. I want to understand your needs better so we can build the perfect solution for you. Can you tell me about your current ordering process?
Customer: Sure, our current process is a bit tedious. We use a mix of spreadsheets and emails to place orders with different suppliers.	Customer: Sure, our current process is a bit tedious. We use a mix of spreadsheets and emails to place orders with different suppliers.
Rajat: That sounds cumbersome. What are the biggest challenges you face with this process?	Rajat: Got it. So, if I understand correctly, you need a more streamlined way to place orders?

Customer: We often have errors in orders, it's time-consuming, and there's no real-time update, which causes delays.	Customer: Yes, that would be helpful.
Rajat: I see. Can you give me an example of a recent issue you faced?	Rajat: Great! Let's talk specifics. What features would you like to see in an ordering system?
Customer: Just last week, we had a supplier miss an order because the email got lost, and we didn't realize it until it was too late.	Customer: It would be nice if we could have a way to save our regular orders and maybe have some kind of tracking for deliveries.
Rajat: That must have been frustrating. How do you currently handle orders for different types of products, like cheese or spices?	Rajat: Excellent! We can definitely add those. What about different types of food? Do you have any preferences on how to order different recipes?
Customer: Well, some products aren't ordered by weight. We might order cheese by the block or certain spices in packets instead of kilograms.	Customer: Well, sometimes we have specific requirements for certain dishes, but generally, we just need a consistent process. For example, some products aren't ordered by weight. We might order cheese by the block or certain spices in packets instead of kilograms.

Rajat: Interesting. How often do these specific requirements come up, and how do you currently manage them?	Rajat: I see. So, it sounds like we need different ordering flows for different recipes and criteria. Anything else?
Customer: They come up fairly often. Right now, we just manually adjust the orders, which can be a hassle.	Customer: Uh, I suppose some customization options for each order might be useful, but we don't want it to be too complicated.
Rajat: It sounds like flexibility and reducing manual adjustments would be beneficial. Are there any other pain points or needs you have with the current system?	Rajat: No problem, we'll make sure to include customization options. What kind of reports do you want to generate from the system?
Customer: Integration with our existing systems would save a lot of time, and a simpler, more intuitive interface would help our team.	Customer: Reports? We haven't really thought about that. Maybe just basic order summaries.
Rajat: Got it. So, integration and ease of use are key. Can you prioritize these needs for me? What would have the biggest impact?	Rajat: Got it. So, detailed analytics and advanced reporting features might not be necessary?
Customer: Streamlining the process and reducing errors	Customer: Yeah, we just need something simple.

would be the top priorities. Integration would come next.	
Rajat: Thanks for sharing that. Any specific user interface preferences or existing systems you want to ensure compatibility with?	Rajat: Understood. How about integration with your existing systems? Is that important?
Customer: As long as it's easy to use and works with our current inventory management system, we're happy.	Customer: Yes, that would be very useful.
Rajat: Perfect. We'll focus on making it user-friendly and compatible with your inventory system. Can you tell me more about how your team uses the inventory management system on a daily basis?	Rajat: Perfect, we'll include that. Do you have any preferences for the user interface design?
Customer: Sure, our team uses it to track stock levels, update item locations, and manage incoming and outgoing shipments.	Customer: As long as it's easy to use, we're happy.
Rajat: And how often do you face issues with your current system's integration, or lack thereof?	Rajat: Got it. I'll make sure it's user-friendly. Any specific color schemes or branding guidelines we should follow?

Customer: Quite often. It's mostly related to manual data entry and syncing delays.	Customer: Not really, we're flexible on that.
Rajat: That sounds like a significant problem. How do these integration issues impact your daily operations?	Rajat: Great, thanks for all the input! This has been very helpful.
Customer: It causes delays and errors in orders, which leads to frustration and lost time.	Customer: Not really, we're flexible on that.
Rajat: I see. Addressing these integration issues will be a priority. Are there any other challenges or areas for improvement you'd like to mention?	
Customer: Real-time updates and notifications would also be great. It would help us stay on top of things without constantly checking the system.	
Rajat: Real-time updates and notifications, got it. Thanks for sharing all these details, they're very helpful. We'll aim to create	

| a solution that addresses these pain points effectively. | |
| Customer: Glad to help. Looking forward to seeing the new system. | |

Exercise

Which conversation would you rate better

1. A
2. B
3. Both are good
4. Both are bad

Based on your selection, write what could be improved in the other conversation?

Based on your selection, what did the interviewer do well in the conversation of your answer?

If a customer mentioned using spreadsheets and emails for their ordering process, what follow-up questions would you ask to understand their pain points better?

> A customer tells you they face issues with manual data entry and syncing delays. How would you address this in your product development plan?

> Write a list of features, that you would develop based on the interviews:

Read after the exercise

Key Mistakes in the Conversation B:

1. Leading Questions: Guided the customer towards specific answers (e.g., "So, if I understand correctly, you need a more streamlined way to place orders?").

2. Assuming Specific Solutions: Jumped to solutions without understanding the problem deeply (e.g., "So, it sounds like we need different ordering flows for different recipes and criteria.").

3. Ignoring Broader Problems: Didn't explore broader issues mentioned by the customer (e.g., spreadsheets and emails indicating integration problems).

4. Overlooking Simplicity: Focused on adding multiple features without considering the need for simplicity (e.g., "No problem, we'll make sure to include customization options.").

5. Lack of Prioritization: Failed to prioritize features based on customer needs (e.g., asking for feature requests without evaluating their importance).

6. Lack of Clarity: Did not seek clarification on vague responses (e.g., "sometimes we have specific requirements for certain dishes").

7. Surface-Level Questions: Did not delve into underlying problems (e.g., "Can you tell me about your current ordering process?" Without following up on pain points).

8. Feature Overload: Suggested unnecessary features (e.g., detailed analytics and advanced reporting).

9. Missing Pain Points: Did not explore specific pain points related to spreadsheets and emails (e.g., errors, inefficiency).

10. Assuming Importance: Assumed certain features were important without confirming their priority (e.g., user interface preferences).

To avoid the pitfalls Rajat encountered, here are some best practices for conducting effective customer interviews:

1. Ask Open-Ended Questions: Encourage customers to share their experiences and pain points without guiding them towards specific answers.

2. Understand the Broader Problem: Focus on understanding the root cause of the customer's issues rather than jumping to specific solutions.

3. Prioritize Simplicity: Ensure the product remains user-friendly and doesn't become overly complex with unnecessary features.

4. Evaluate Feature Importance: Prioritize features based on their impact on the user experience and overall business goals.

5. Iterative Feedback: Continuously gather feedback and iterate on the product design to ensure it meets user needs effectively.

By learning from Rajat's mistakes, product managers can develop better interviewing techniques, leading to products that truly meet customer needs and drive business success.

Chapter 31.
Product Experimentations

How do you know which product ideas are worth building? It is highly unlikely that you know which ideas will work for sure. If this were the case, then the majority of businesses would be highly successful. It is only with certain probability that one can start building a product. And in reality, waiting too long for a perfect answer is a lost war.

Product experimentation is the process of testing ideas or hypotheses to measure their impacts—in this case, on customer satisfaction and product performance. What the users say and what they actually do can be two different things. Lot of times customers themselves don't know why they take certain decisions they actually do. In the psychology of product management, you read that people are not actually logical when they make decisions. This leads to a number of issues for product managers. One wrong insight can lead to wasted months of work. Users might express a preference for feature X, yet when given the choice, they might overwhelmingly choose feature Y. You can find this example in the kind of reels and videos that get viral. It is usually the kind of videos you would generally not decide - when thinking logically - to put in your choice that you end up enjoying. What is critical to understand here is no matter how much you think you know about the customer; actual user behavior can be different.

This discrepancy necessitates rigorous experimentation and hypothesis testing to validate assumptions and understand true user behavior. The following chapters cover the principles of designing effective experiments to uncover these insights. There are 100's of simple ways to validate your product. The efficacy of each of them depends on the use case. One strategy can be great for a specific use case but is a complete failure for the other.

Hypothesis testing in product management starts with forming a clear, testable hypothesis. A well-structured hypothesis follows this format: "We believe [specific change] will result in [expected outcome] for [target audience]." Example: We believe that adding a one-click checkout option will increase the purchase completion rate for mobile users. To test this hypothesis, an experiment must be designed where one group of users experiences the one-click checkout option (the experimental group), while another group continues with the existing checkout process (the control group).

There are certain methodologies (or experiment design) which if done correctly lead to products that customers love. This section details these designs in detail and how each of them should be executed. At the core of each of these are simple defined steps

1. Define the Objective: Clearly outline what you aim to learn or achieve. This objective should align with your overall product goals. Example: Increase the purchase completion rate.

2. Select the Metrics: Identify key performance indicators (KPIs) that will measure the success of the experiment. Example: Purchase completion rate, time taken to complete the purchase, user satisfaction scores.

3. Choose the Experimental Design: Decide between A/B testing, multivariate testing, or other methods based on the hypothesis. Example: Compare the existing checkout process (A) with the one-click checkout process (B).

4. Randomize and Control: Ensure that users are randomly assigned to experimental and control groups to eliminate biases.

5. Conduct the Experiment: Implement the changes and run the experiment for a sufficient period to gather meaningful data. Example: Run the test for two weeks to gather enough data for statistical significance.

6. Analyze the Results: Use statistical methods to determine if the observed differences are significant. Example: Compare the purchase completion rates of both groups using statistical tests.

7. Iterate or Implement: Based on the results, decide whether to roll out the change to all users, iterate on the experiment, or discard the hypothesis. Example: If the one-click checkout significantly improves completion rates, plan for a full rollout.

Let's take an example of a social media platform. Suppose the objective is to increase the user engagement of video content. We need to design an experiment to understand which videos to promote. Users might claim they prefer educational content, yet data often shows that entertaining, sometimes trivial videos are the ones that go viral.

Hypothesis: Introducing a "Recommended for You" section based on user behavior will increase video engagement rates.

1. Objective: Increase overall video engagement rates.
2. Metrics: Engagement rate (likes, shares, comments), time spent watching videos.
3. Experimental Design: A/B test with a control group experiencing the regular feed and an experimental group seeing the new "Recommended for You" section.
4. Randomization: Randomly assign users to either group.
5. Conduct the Experiment: Run the test for a month.
6. Analyze the Results: Compare engagement metrics between the two groups.
7. Decision: If the recommended section shows higher engagement, consider implementing it permanently.

Effective product management relies on the ability to validate assumptions through well-designed experiments. By understanding and predicting user behavior accurately, product managers can make data-driven decisions that align with actual user preferences, leading to successful product outcomes. We will discuss some of the experiments in detail in the next few chapters. An exhaustive list of the product experiments is available in the resource section.

Chapter 32.
A/B Testing

A/B testing involves testing two versions of the same thing with a slight variation to be tested with the users. Imagine your favorite ice cream store wants to launch a new ice cream flavor. Before starting the mass production of ice creams, the store is confused about which flavor will people like more? With some surveys and research, they found that people generally have a liking for either mango or grape flavor but one cannot be chosen for sure. So, it decides to run a small test with actual ice cream with actual people. The store invites two hundred people for the free ice cream test. They randomly give mango flavor to one set of people and grape flavor to another set of people. The flavor with more people liking it wins the test and ultimately gets chosen for mass production. This activity not only chose the best ice cream, it saved a lot of money which would have got wasted if the wrong ice-cream was chosen for mass production.

A/B tests in the web world are similar. You test two different versions of the web page with the user with a defined outcome. Product managers use this to test the variation of the heading, button, color on the landing page to gauge the conversion. These tests are applicable in a variety of situations starting from website optimization to marketing to testing product features.

Common Use Cases for A/B Testing

Website Optimization: Think of A/B testing as a way to make your website more like your favorite store—easy to navigate and full of things you love to buy. Product managers often use A/B testing to experiment with different layouts, menus, and buttons to figure out what makes it easier for users to find what they're looking for. For example, you might test two versions of the checkout page to see which one leads to more purchases. The version that helps more people complete their purchases wins.

Email Marketing: Imagine getting two emails from your favorite brand, each with a different subject line. One says, "Big Sale Inside!" and the other says, "Exclusive Discounts Just for You." By sending both versions to different groups of people, the company can see which subject line gets more people to open the email. Then, they can test the content inside, like different images or buttons, to see which version leads to more clicks and sales. This way, they're not guessing what works—they know what actually gets more people excited to open and engage with their emails.

Landing Page Design: Let's say you visit a landing page for a new product. In one version, the main headline says, "Buy Now and Save!" while another version says, "Limited Time Offer!" A/B testing allows the product team to see which version makes more people click the "Buy" button. Maybe it's the layout of the images, the color of the buttons, or the placement of the call-to-action. By testing these small changes, the team can figure out what turns more visitors into customers, just like tweaking an ice cream shop's window display to bring more people inside.

Product Features: Another powerful way you can use A/B testing to test new features, like a personalized recommendations section. The product team might run an A/B test to see if this new feature actually makes users happier or more engaged. One group of users sees the app with the new feature, and another group sees the app without it. The team can then measure things like how much time users spend on the app or how often they use the new feature. If the group with the new feature is more active and satisfied, they'll know they're onto something.

Marketing Campaigns: Picture two different ads for the same product—one uses bright colors and bold text, while the other uses a softer, more subtle design. By running an A/B test, the marketing team can figure out which ad gets more clicks, purchases, or sign-ups. They might also test different targeting strategies, like showing one ad to younger users and another to an older audience. This way, they can fine-tune their campaigns and make sure every marketing dollar counts, just like figuring out which billboard or flyer gets more people into a new store.

Some of the common mistakes while designing an A/B

Not Enough Data: Imagine running a taste test for two new ice cream flavors but only asking five people for their opinion. It's not enough to know which flavor people really prefer. The same thing happens in A/B testing. If you don't have enough users testing your versions, the results won't be reliable. You might think one version is better, but it could just be a random chance.

Too Many Changes at Once: Think about trying two new ice cream flavors but also changing the packaging and the price at the same time. If people like one version better, you won't know whether it was the flavor, the packaging, or the price they preferred. In A/B testing, it's important to change just one thing at a time so you can be sure what made the difference.

Stopping the Test Too Soon: Imagine you give out samples of a new ice cream and, after just a few people say they love it, you decide to launch it everywhere. What if you waited a little longer and found out more people actually preferred the other flavor? In A/B testing, some teams stop as soon as they see a positive result, but the early data might not be reliable. You need to wait long enough to be sure.

Tracking the Wrong Results: Imagine you ask people which ice cream looks best but don't ask which one tastes best. You're focusing on something that doesn't really matter for your goal. In A/B testing, if you track things like how many people visit your page (page views) instead of how many people buy something (conversions), you won't get the insights you need. Focus on the right outcomes.

Today there are many tools available to help product managers run these tests. Tools like GetSiteControl and VWO are great tools for such experiments. It gives flexibility in the hands of the product managers to quickly test their hypothesis. Getsitecontrol gives you the ability to put popup, floating icons and notification bar. VWO gives you access to controlling the UI elements and embedding forms, headers and other advanced UI elements. Both serve their purpose well and of great use for product managers.

Chapter 33.
Minimum Viable Product (MVP)

The full form of MVP is the minimum viable product. What this means is the product is viable meaning able to work successfully to achieve the desired outcome. If you create an MVP which does not fulfill a function or result in an outcome or solve user pain points, then it is not a minimum viable product. Apart from solving a problem, it should work independently and successfully to achieve the desired result.

Another question that comes to mind is why MVP? Simply save you time and money. Rather than spending a significant amount of resources on building a complete product and then finding out that there are no buyers of the same, it is often sensible to first create a small working solution to test out with your users. Many startups go shut because of this. At RCorp, I did not understand this. We always thought that the product is useless without feature x and feature y. We never went to the users. As with all products, the product was never complete and we never felt that the users would use it. What we were missing is the idea of MVP. When I look back now, I realize that the most important thing was to bring the product in front of the user; make them use it and build from there. We were forever featuring paralysis which ultimately led to failure of most products.

Many of us think of MVP as a major project itself. This is where most of us get wrong. MVPs are supposed to be quick and give your insight quickly. Creating a holiday package is a fairly tedious task even for advanced portals. Travel agents have a habit of submitting the requirement on emails. We launched a product for the same where agents could create and customize the requirement. After a year of working on the product being live, we wanted to improve the number of quotes created by the agent. There was a feeling that if we remove the resistance of filling the form and allow copy paste of the requirement, it would have a lot more traction. We wanted to test this idea and hence created an exit intent pop-up; it led to approximately 2% conversion. This was a fairly quick MVP made possible with getsitecontrol.

I think the best way to create an MVP today is to think that you are in early 2000 and you have an idea. How do you create a prototype of the product that you actually want to launch? Suppose you are an edtech startup. With your experience working with teachers, parents, and students, you realize that an on-demand worksheet generator would be a great product to launch. How do you create an MVP for the same? Before committing to create a full-fledged product, you would just launch a small product on WhatsApp where customers can post their requirement and you revert back with a worksheet say in 30 mins. If there is enough traction for such a product and customers are ready to pay for the same then maybe you move ahead with the iterations. This simple product would help you learn about how to collect the worksheet requirements, what kind of questions teachers or parents need and much more about the market.

When the online commerce was in its infancy the food startup Zomato collected the offline menu and digitized it and made it available. This simple idea was a good enough prototype to test the demand. Though it required a lot of effort and tech for that time, it is a good MVP approach in the present day to test an idea.

At travclan we created one of the biggest MVP through Google Sheets. We created calculators for creating packages for different destinations. This MVP ran for more than a year before a final product was developed. What we did next was not create a fully functional product but create a version of the same using wordpress in a similar hacky way. All these efforts helped us keep the business running while helping us test our ideas with real users and accumulate our learning. As a result, over a period of 2 years it helped to get a good understanding of Holiday products and faster iterations.

One of the ways to create MVP is the Sprint process, developed by Jake Knapp. It is a five-day method designed to solve critical business problems and test new ideas through rapid prototyping and user feedback. It involves intense focus on developing the prototype with core people involved. Here's a summary of the process:

1. Day 1 (Monday) – Map: The team defines the problem and sets a long-term goal. They create a detailed map of the challenge, identifying key aspects that need focus. The day ends with selecting a target area to address during the sprint.

2. Day 2 (Tuesday) – Sketch: Participants individually sketch out competing solutions based on the insights from Day 1. They focus on creativity and finding the best ways to tackle the problem.

3. Day 3 (Wednesday) – Decide: The team reviews all the sketches and votes on the best solutions. By the end of the day, they select a winning concept, creating a storyboard to flesh out the chosen idea.

4. Day 4 (Thursday) – Prototype: A realistic but low-effort prototype of the solution is created. The goal is to make something testable, simulating a real product without investing too much time in perfection.

5. Day 5 (Friday) – Test: The team tests the prototype on real users. Feedback is gathered to learn what works, what doesn't, and whether the concept is viable. This helps guide the next steps, whether it's iterating on the idea or moving in a new direction.

Whether you follow the Sprint process, Google sheet, Google forms or any other form of automation, it is important to note that MVP should deliver some value or solve user problems. Moreover, they are supposed to be quick.

Chapter 34.
Design Prototypes

After you understand the problem, the next step is to work with product designers to come up with possible solutions. Designers will create mockups or prototypes that show what the solution might look like and how it could work. These early designs help you visualize the product and test your ideas.

To start, make sure you explain the problem clearly to the designers. Share the key issues you're trying to solve, the needs of your users, and any insights from your research. This helps the designers create mockups that are focused and useful.

Once the mockups are ready, test them with real users. This step is essential to find out if the solution actually works for the people it's meant to help. During these tests, observe how users interact with the prototype. Notice where they get confused, make mistakes, or hesitate. These moments can reveal areas that need improvement.

User feedback is a valuable tool for uncovering problems with your solution. Sometimes, it may even challenge your original ideas about how to solve the issue. You should be open to rethinking your approach based on what you learn. Ask questions like, "Does this design solve the main problem?" or "Are there new issues we didn't expect?"

Finally, use the feedback to refine the prototype. This process of designing, testing, and improving helps you create a product that truly meets the needs of your users. It's better to find and fix problems in the early stages than after the product is built. Prototypes allow you to test ideas quickly and ensure your solution is on the right track.

Chapter 35.
Beta Invitation

When launching a new product or feature, beta invitations can be a powerful tool to validate ideas and gather valuable user feedback early in the development process. A beta invitation allows you to test interest and usability before committing significant resources to building the full product. By combining this with a clear funnel, such as driving users to a sign-up page, you can define success criteria for the experiment and use the results to make informed decisions.

Dropbox, a cloud storage service, used beta invitations to test their product concept and prioritize features. Founder Drew Houston shared a video demo of Dropbox on forums like Hacker News, sparking early interest. People who were intrigued by the demo signed up to be part of the beta testing program. Dropbox followed this up with surveys and polls to gather deeper insights into user needs and pain points.

Through the beta program, Dropbox was able to refine its product in several ways:

- **Feature Prioritization:** Surveys showed that some features, like an unlimited "undo" option, were not widely used. This helped Dropbox focus on features that mattered more to users, saving resources while aligning the product with real needs.

- **Improving the User Experience:** Feedback from beta testers highlighted pain points, allowing Dropbox to make adjustments that enhanced usability. This process balanced quantitative data, like analytics, with the qualitative insights from users.

- **Referral Program Optimization:** Beta testers played a crucial role in shaping Dropbox's iconic referral program. By listening to user feedback, Dropbox tweaked the program to offer incentives that appealed to their audience. This refined approach resulted in explosive growth as users eagerly referred friends to the platform.

Similarly, Clubhouse, an audio-based social networking app, took a different but equally effective approach to beta invitations. By restricting access through an invitation-only system, Clubhouse created a sense of exclusivity that drove user interest and engagement.

Here's how the beta invitation model worked for Clubhouse:

- Invitation-Only Access: Early users were given a limited number of invites to share with friends. This scarcity made the app feel special and desirable.

- High-Profile Users: Clubhouse reached out to celebrities, influencers, and thought leaders, giving them early access. These individuals brought credibility and helped generate buzz about the platform.

- Feedback Loop: A smaller, invitation-only user base allowed Clubhouse to manage server loads effectively and refine the app based on real-world usage.

- Organic Growth: Users invited friends they thought would enjoy the app, creating a network of engaged, like-minded individuals.

- Exclusivity and FOMO: The invitation model amplified the fear of missing out (FOMO), encouraging people to seek invitations actively.

As a result of this strategy, Clubhouse gained rapid popularity and built a loyal, engaged community. The feedback collected during this period helped the developers refine the app's features and position it as a leader in audio-based social networking.

Now let's imagine you're the product manager of QuickMeet, a tool for scheduling meetings, and you want to validate the interest in a new feature: Auto-Schedule Meetings, which automatically finds the best meeting times based on participants' availability and preferences.

Here's how you could set up a beta invitation experiment:

1. Create a Demo: Develop a simple video or interactive prototype that explains how the feature works. Share this with potential users to spark interest.

2. Set Up a Sign-Up Funnel: Build a landing page where users can sign up to test the feature. Track how many people complete the sign-up process.

3. Send Invitations: Invite a small group of users to test the feature in a controlled beta environment. Ensure the invited users reflect your target audience.

4. Gather Feedback: Use surveys and interviews to understand what users like, dislike, and want improved. Ask questions about usability and whether the feature meets their needs.

5. Measure Engagement: Track how users interact with the feature. Are they scheduling meetings more efficiently? Are there any issues or pain points?

6. Refine the Feature: Use the feedback to prioritize changes and improvements before launching the feature to a wider audience.

Beta invitations are not just about building a product—they're about building a relationship with your consumers. By listening to feedback and iteration based on real needs, you can create something truly valuable that resonates with your audience.

Resources

Product Experiments List

1. Landing Page Test: Create a simple landing page describing the product concept. Use a call-to-action (CTA) button such as "Sign Up" or "Learn More" to measure interest.

2. A/B Testing: Use A/B testing tools to present two different versions of a feature or design to users and compare engagement metrics.

3. Customer Interviews: Conduct quick, informal interviews with potential users to gather qualitative feedback on the product idea.

4. Surveys and Polls: Deploy a brief survey to your target audience to gauge interest and gather feedback on specific aspects of the product.

5. Social Media Ad Campaigns: Run targeted ads on social media platforms to measure click-through rates and engagement with the product concept.

6. Email Campaigns: Send out a teaser email to a segment of your mailing list and track open and click-through rates to assess interest.

7. Prototype Testing: Develop a low-fidelity prototype and conduct usability testing sessions to observe how users interact with the product.

8. Crowdsourcing Feedback: Use platforms like UserTesting or TryMyUI to get quick feedback from a diverse group of users.

9. Explainer Video: Create a short explainer video about the product and measure engagement metrics such as views, likes, and shares.

10. Pre-Order Page: Set up a pre-order page for the product to see if users are willing to commit financially before the product is fully developed.

11. Feature Voting: Allow users to vote on potential features or aspects of the product to prioritize development based on actual user demand.

12. Chatbot Interaction: Use a chatbot on your website to engage visitors in conversation about the product and gather insights based on their responses.

13. Mock Sales Calls: Simulate sales calls with potential customers to pitch the product and gauge their reactions and interest.

14. Referral Program: Launch a referral program to see if current users are willing to recommend the product to others.

15. Webinar: Host a webinar to introduce the product concept and engage with potential users in real-time, collecting feedback and questions.

16. Beta Testing: Release a beta version of the product to a small group of users and gather detailed feedback on their experience.

17. Pop-Up Surveys: Implement pop-up surveys on your website or app to capture immediate feedback from users.

18. Concept Testing: Use tools like PickFu to present different product concepts to a panel of users and get instant feedback on which concept resonates more.

19. Price Sensitivity Analysis: Test different price points to see how price affects user interest and willingness to pay.

20. Online Forums and Communities: Engage with online communities and forums related to your product niche to gather insights and feedback from active members.

21. Heatmaps: Use tools like Hotjar or Crazy Egg to analyze where users click and how they navigate on your website, providing insights into what captures their attention.

22. Time on Task Analysis: Observe how long it takes for users to complete specific tasks within a prototype or beta version, indicating usability and efficiency.

23. Interactive Demos: Create an interactive demo or guided tour of the product and measure user engagement and completion rates.

24. Customer Journey Mapping: Develop a detailed customer journey map and validate it by asking potential users to walk through the steps and provide feedback.

25. Content Marketing Test: Publish a blog post or article related to the product concept and measure engagement metrics such as views, shares, and comments.

26. Competitive Analysis: Compare user interest in your product against competitors by offering similar features and gathering comparative feedback.

27. Gamified Surveys: Design a survey with gamified elements to increase participation and collect more engaging feedback.

28. Online Focus Groups: Conduct a virtual focus group session to discuss the product idea and gather in-depth feedback from participants.

29. User Personas: Create detailed user personas and validate them by interviewing real users to see how closely they match.

30. AB Testing Emails: Send two versions of an email campaign with different subject lines or content to measure which one generates more interest.

31. Quizzes and Assessments: Develop a quiz related to your product's problem space and share it with users to see if they find it relevant and engaging.

32. Interactive Polls: Use social media platforms to run quick polls and gather instant feedback from your audience.

33. Micro Surveys: Implement one-question surveys on your website or app to gather quick insights on specific features or concepts.

34. Virtual Reality (VR) Demos: Create a VR demo of the product if applicable and measure user engagement and feedback.

35. Flash Sales: Run a flash sale or limited-time offer to test price sensitivity and urgency.

36. User Diaries: Ask a small group of users to keep a diary of their interactions with the product over a day and provide detailed feedback.

37. Click-Through Prototypes: Develop a clickable prototype using tools like InVision or Figma and conduct usability tests to gather feedback.

38. Chat Room Discussions: Set up a chat room or Slack channel for potential users to discuss the product concept and provide real-time feedback.

39. Social Listening: Monitor social media and online forums for mentions of your product or problem space to gather unsolicited feedback.

40. Usability Studies: Conduct usability studies where users complete tasks while thinking aloud, providing insights into their thought process.

41. Content Drip Campaign: Create a series of automated emails that provide value and slowly introduce the product, measuring engagement and conversion rates.

42. Referral Codes: Provide unique referral codes to a small group of users and track how effectively they spread the word about your product.

43. Freemium Model Test: Offer a free version of the product with limited features and measure how many users upgrade to the paid version.

44. Mystery Shopping: Hire mystery shoppers to test the customer service and user experience provided by your product or service.

45. Interactive Webinars: Host a live interactive webinar where participants can ask questions and engage with the product concept in real-time.

46. In-App Messaging: Use in-app messaging to prompt users for feedback on specific features or concepts.

47. Digital Prototyping: Use digital prototyping tools to create a high-fidelity prototype and conduct remote usability tests.

48. Net Promoter Score (NPS): Send a quick NPS survey to gauge user satisfaction and likelihood to recommend the product.

49. Exit Surveys: Implement an exit survey on your website to capture feedback from users as they leave the site.

50. Online Contests: Run an online contest related to your product to generate buzz and gather feedback on the concept.

51. Video Testimonials: Request video testimonials from early users or beta testers to capture authentic feedback and social proof.

52. Influencer Partnerships: Partner with influencers to promote the product and gather feedback from their audience.

53. Discount Offers: Offer a limited-time discount to see if price incentives increase user interest and conversion rates.

54. Product Hunt Launch: Launch your product on Product Hunt to gather feedback from the tech community and measure interest.

55. Voice of the Customer Programs: Implement a Voice of the Customer program to continuously gather feedback from users.

56. Scenario-Based Testing: Create specific scenarios for users to complete using your product and gather feedback on their experience.

57. Augmented Reality (AR) Previews: Use AR to allow users to preview the product in their environment and measure engagement.

58. Expert Reviews: Send the product concept to industry experts or bloggers for review and gather their feedback.

59. Concept Testing with Interactive Mockups: Use tools like Axure or Marvel to create interactive mockups and gather feedback through user testing sessions.

60. Storyboards: Create storyboards depicting different use cases and ask potential users to provide feedback on the scenarios.

61. Affiliate Marketing Test: Set up an affiliate marketing program to see if partners are willing to promote your product and how well it converts.

62. Clickable Email Signatures: Add a CTA related to the product in your email signature and track clicks to measure interest.

63. Scratch Card Promotion: Use a digital scratch card promotion to engage users and see what rewards motivate them the most.

64. User Reviews on Mockup Sites: Post product mockups on sites like Behance or Dribble and gather feedback from the design community.

65. Mini White Paper: Write a short white paper on the problem your product solves and distribute it to gauge interest.

66. Personalized Onboarding: Create a personalized onboarding experience for new users and measure engagement and feedback.

67. Influencer Q&A Sessions: Partner with influencers to host Q&A sessions about your product and collect questions and feedback from their audience.

68. Mobile App Previews: If applicable, create a preview version of your mobile app and distribute it to gather user feedback.

69. Feature Teasers on social media: Share teasers of upcoming features on social media and measure engagement to gauge interest.

70. Interactive Infographics: Develop interactive infographics that explain your product's benefits and track user interactions.

71. User-Generated Content Campaigns: Encourage users to create content related to your product and gather feedback through their creations.

72. Collaborative Road mapping: Involve users in the product roadmap planning process and gather their input on priorities.

73. Quick Polls During Webinars: Conduct quick polls during webinars to gather real-time feedback from participants.

74. Exclusive Beta Invitations: Send out exclusive invitations for a beta test to gauge interest and gather early feedback.

75. Competitor Product Testing: Have users test competitor products and provide feedback on what they like or dislike compared to your concept.

76. Customer Service Chats: Use customer service chat logs to identify recurring issues or suggestions related to the product.

77. Gamified Feedback Collection: Create a gamified feedback collection process where users earn points or rewards for providing insights.

78. Test New User Experiences (NUX): Experiment with different NUX flows to see which one retains users better.

79. Social Proof Experiment: Test different forms of social proof (testimonials, user counts, endorsements) on your website to see which drives more conversions.

80. AI Chatbots for Feedback: Implement AI chatbots to interact with users and gather feedback on their experience with the product.

81. Interactive Product Walkthroughs: Create interactive walkthroughs that guide users through the product's features and measure their reactions.

82. Website Exit Intent Popups: Use exit intent popups to capture feedback from users who are about to leave your website.

83. Concept Art Sharing: Share concept art of the product on forums and social media to gather early impressions.

84. User Need Surveys: Conduct surveys focused on understanding user needs and how well your product idea addresses them.

85. Limited-Edition Releases: Offer limited-edition versions of the product to test scarcity and exclusivity as motivators.

86. Targeted LinkedIn Ads: Run targeted ads on LinkedIn to professionals in your target market and measure engagement.

87. Early Access Rewards: Offer rewards for early access sign-ups and track which incentives are most appealing.

88. Prototype Challenges: Host challenges where users compete to provide the best feedback on a prototype.

89. Subscription Box Test: If applicable, create a subscription box related to your product and gauge interest.

90. Influencer-Generated Content: Have influencers create content around your product and measure the resulting engagement.

91. Early Bird Pricing: Offer early bird pricing to see if discounts drive early adoption and interest.

92. Dynamic Content Testing: Test dynamic content on your website that changes based on user behavior to see what resonates most.

93. Interactive Workshops: Host virtual workshops where users can interact with the product concept and provide feedback.

94. Predictive Analytics: Use predictive analytics to identify trends and user behavior that can validate product assumptions.

95. Online Competitions: Run online competitions related to your product's niche to engage users and gather feedback.

96. User Feedback through Push Notifications: Send push notifications asking for quick feedback on specific features or concepts.

97. Feedback Widgets on Websites: Implement feedback widgets that allow users to rate and comment on specific parts of your website or app.

98. Voice Feedback Collection: Use voice feedback tools to gather audio comments from users about your product.

99. Augmented Reality Surveys: If applicable, use AR surveys to engage users in an immersive feedback experience.

100. Educational Webinars: Host educational webinars about the problem space your product addresses and gather feedback on the presented solutions.

101. Interactive Polls in Stories: Use Instagram or Facebook Stories to run interactive polls and measure engagement.

102. NPS Follow-Up Questions: After collecting NPS scores, ask follow-up questions to gather deeper insights into user satisfaction.

103. User Experience Mapping Workshops: Conduct workshops where users map out their ideal experience with your product.

104. Crowdfunding Campaigns: Launch a crowdfunding campaign to validate interest and gather feedback from backers.

105. Feedback through QR Codes: Place QR codes in relevant locations or materials that direct users to a feedback form.

106. User Forums: Create a forum for users to discuss the product and provide feedback in a community setting.

107. Customer Advisory Boards: Set up a customer advisory board to provide ongoing feedback and insights on your product development.

108. Demo Day Events: Host demo day events where users can try out the product and provide real-time feedback.

109. Online Surveys with Rewards: Offer rewards for completing online surveys to increase participation and gather detailed feedback.

110. Product Naming Contests: Run contests to crowdsource names for your product and gauge interest through participation.

111. Influencer Takeovers: Have influencers take over your social media accounts to promote the product and collect feedback from their followers.

112. SMS Feedback Campaigns: Use SMS campaigns to gather quick feedback from users on specific product features or concepts.

113. Virtual Reality Focus Groups: Conduct VR focus groups to immerse users in the product experience and gather detailed feedback.

114. Customer Satisfaction Index (CSI): Measure customer satisfaction through a CSI survey and analyze the results to validate your product hypothesis.

115. Storytelling Videos: Create storytelling videos about how your product solves a problem and measure viewer engagement.

116. Podcasts for Feedback: Host a podcast episode discussing the product concept and invite listener feedback.

117. Early Access Quizzes: Use quizzes to determine if users qualify for early access and gather data on their preferences.

118. Influencer-Led Surveys: Have influencers share surveys with their followers to gather broader feedback.

119. Trial Periods: Offer free trial periods to see how many users convert to paid customers after the trial ends.

120. Interactive Tutorials: Develop interactive tutorials that guide users through the product and collect feedback on their experience.

References

1. **Chapter 34: Dropbox example:**
   a. https://buckfiftymba.com/what-you-dont-know-about-dropboxs-growth-to-10-billion/
   b. https://mocktheagency.com/content/the-rise-of-dropbox-how-white-papers-and-smart-marketing-strategies-catapulted-the-company-to-success/

2. **Chapter 3: Power of data**
   a. https://info.amplitude.com/rs/138-CDN-550/images/The%20Amplitude%20Guide%20to%20Product%20Metrics.pdf
   b. https://amplitude.com/blog/product-metrics-guide
   c. https://info.amplitude.com/rs/138-CDN-550/images/Product%20Analytics%20For%20Dummies.pdf
   d. https://mixpanel.com/content/guide-to-product-analytics/chapter_1/
   e. https://assets.ctfassets.net/6nwv0fapso8r/7yjCkTEHPLpjDPbqDkuRXS/46680d951cc704feb80bf2a52d34e15e/The-Product-Analytics-Economy.pdf?mkt_tok=ODgwLURWRi0yMjQAAAGU6ubk9Gg7DCWctdnhpJRE93nIYBT9LW79x5BCnAKWYpIe6ZmphMP3bxGjaICoEHtpYB_cxrn5XtFwTas6n8RKpJiqfURjRk5_iwWEZxI

3. **Chapter 4: Feature Priortization**
   a. https://productschool.com/blog/product-fundamentals/ultimate-guide-product-prioritization

b. https://www.kanomodel.com/wp-content/uploads/2015/08/KanoArticle_2013.pdf

4. **Chapter 6: Eroding Goals**

   a. https://proceedings.systemdynamics.org/2007/proceed/papers/BRAUN489.pdf

   b. https://proceedings.systemdynamics.org/2003/proceed/PAPERS/361.pdf

   c. https://thesystemsthinker.com/systems-archetypes-i-diagnosing-systemic-issues-and-designing-interventions/

   d. https://www.spaceline.org/united-states-manned-space-flight/challenger-legacy-index/the-challenger-tragedy/

5. **Chapter 22: Cognitive Load**

   a. https://arrow.tudublin.ie/cgi/viewcontent.cgi?article=1354&context=scschcomcon

6. **Chapter 30: Product Experimentation**

   a. https://itamargilad.com/wp-content/uploads/2022/01/Testing-Product-Ideas-Handbook.pdf

7. **Kahneman, D. (2011). Thinking, fast and slow. Farrar, Straus and Giroux.**